Successful SEO And Search Marketing In A Week

Nick Smith

I'd like to dedicate this book to: my beautiful and infinitely patient wife Shirley, without whom I would be nothing – I love you; my children Jemma and Deanna, who keep me young (but sometimes make me feel old); my mum and dad, for teaching me that there are no shortcuts in life – just work smart and hard and you'll get there; to my brother Matt, who reminds me to keep doing what you love; Yanik Silver, who gave me my first break – thanks, buddy; to all the crazy people in DevGroup – here's to another seven years of helping each other; to Cliff Fontenot, whose input was invaluable during the writing of this book – multumesc.

Nick Smith runs a successful online marketing consultancy, advising companies how to increase sales and profits using the power of the Internet and by leveraging forgotten assets hidden in their business. One of the leading direct-response marketing consultants in the UK, Nick devises effective traffic strategies using a combination of paid marketing sources, search engine optimization and social media marketing.

Nick is also the author of *Successful Social Media Marketing* in this series of 'In A Week' business books. Visit his website at http://nickthegeek.com

Successful SEO And Search Marketing

Nick Smith

www.inaweek.co.uk

Teach® Yourself

IN A WEEK

First published in Great Britain in 2013 by Hodder & Stoughton. An Hachette UK company.

First published in US in 2013 by The McGraw-Hill Companies, Inc.

This edition published 2013

Typeset by Cenveo® Publisher Services.

Printed and bound in Great Britain by CPI Group (UK) Ltd, Croydon CRO 4YY.

Hodder & Stoughton policy is to use papers that are natural, renewable and recyclable products and made from wood grown in sustainable forests. The logging and manufacturing processes are expected to conform to the environmental regulations of the country of origin.

Hodder & Stoughton Ltd

338 Euston Road

London NW1 3BH

www.hodder.co.uk

Also available in ebook

Contents

Introduction

You've made a fantastic decision in purchasing this guide to the sometimes baffling world of search engine optimization (SEO) and search engine marketing (SEM). My goal with this book is not to try and teach you every single thing about SEO and SEM. Instead, I want to give you a solid grasp of the fundamentals so you can get your website content found by the search engines and run paid advertising campaigns, driving visitors to your web pages and ultimately generating revenue. You'll be able to do all this in just seven days, with each chapter taking just one or two hours to read.

Contrary to popular belief, SEO and SEM are not too complex for 'mere mortals' to understand and you don't need to spend a fortune on hiring an SEO/SEM expert. I want to strip away as much of the mystique from SEO and SEM as possible, so that you have enough knowledge of all the basics and the terminology to be able to understand the 'techiest' of traffic geeks and even have a conversation with them. We'll uncover the meaning of the jargon and acronyms you need to know, such as pay-per-click advertising (PPC), backlinking, social signals and algorithms.

The challenge for you is to read a chapter each day, get a grasp of the material, take the mini-test at the end to help get it all straight in your mind and then take action on what you've learned. You may have to revisit the material a day or two later, but by the end of the week you'll have a good overview of the subject and know enough to know what you're not clear on, so that you can go back over the information in the book and fill in the gaps if you need to.

This book is not a 'magic button' or an immediate fix for any traffic problems you have. If you're looking for a way to get a free, instant, never-ending stream of visitors to your website, all throwing money at you, you're going to be disappointed. You won't find it because it doesn't exist so, if this is what you hoped for, please put this book back and leave it for someone with more realistic expectations.

What this book *will* do for you is teach you how to structure your website to deliver what the search engines are looking for and thus promote it to the world. If you understand the principles in this book and follow them to their logical completion, you'll see opportunities that even I haven't thought of. I know it may seem far-fetched now, but – trust me – it's true. The web is an ever-evolving thing that changes alarmingly fast but, if you follow the guidelines and principles in this book, you'll never be left with less traffic coming to your site. You can *only* gain from any changes in the future.

I would love to hear your stories. You can email me at: nickthegeek@gmail.com

Nick Smith

http://nickthegeek.com

SUNDAY

An introduction to search engines and SEO

Welcome to the first day of the rest of your traffic-generating life!

So you have (or want to build) a website. Whether it's a blog, an e-commerce store, an information centre, a niche-specific portal, a company website or any combination thereof, you are probably wondering about the best ways to encourage people to visit your site.

You've probably heard that you have to 'SEO' it to get traffic from users via the search engines and to get yourself some real business. You've bought this book to find out more about what exactly that is and, more specifically, to get that information in only a week.

SEO does not have to be a mysterious code or formula. Today you will find out:

- what SEO is
- what the search engines *really* want
- why you need to SEO at all.

We'll then tell you a little about the layout of the web as it stands now and how to get started.

What exactly is SEO?

Simply put, SEO is the practice of optimizing each page on your website so that it will show as high up the list as possible in the search engine results pages (SERPs) for a particular keyword.

A keyword can be an individual word but it is more likely to be a phrase that a person types into a search engine to get a set of results. The phrase 'underwater cat juggling videos' is a keyword just as much as 'where can I find an emergency plumber in Hoboken New Jersey'.

The higher your website's page shows up in the search engine results for a keyword, all things being equal, the more people will click that link to your web page, come to your website and buy your products, ring for a free quote or whatever you determine to be your most wanted action (MWA). It is important to keep your MWA in your mind at all times, as this is the whole point of your traffic generation efforts.

It sounds simple, but the reality is a little more complicated when we consider how to get noticed.

What do search engines want?

What exactly do search engines want? How do they decide what to rank, and where? Do they even really know? Well, yes and no.

Any honest SEO expert out there, if you get them in a back room (and after they have searched you for hidden microphones), will tell you that we really don't know *exactly* what the search engines want. We know what they *say* they want, but the actual formulas each search engine uses (the computer algorithms) for precisely how and where they rank each of the web pages on your site are kept secret, to try to minimize the ability of unscrupulous people to 'game' their results.

Not only are all the ranking formulas for each search engine kept secret, but each search engine also has a different formula, which is changed and refined on almost a daily basis.

What the search engines say they want basically boils down to one thing: user experience. They want their users to have a good experience. This is where *exactly* what they want becomes less relevant. When Jane goes online and types in her search query for 'best cat food recipe', they want her to get just that: a listing of web pages that each contain information directly related to 'best cat food recipe'.

They don't want Jane to find someone who merely saw a good opportunity to make some money and made their site look to engines as if it was the place for 'best cat food recipe' but – when she clicks on it – it offers nothing but poor-quality information covered in advertising banners. (This happens a lot!)

The question you might now be asking yourself is, 'If I write, design and build an amazing site that delivers the perfect user experience and that is all they really want, is SEO necessary?'

Why do SEO at all?

You might think that, if you provide an amazing user experience, the search engines will find you eventually. This may be true, but it is not a guarantee. Being a search engine is like being a person walking into the Dallas Cowboys' stadium at half-time and told to pick the best fan. You may be the best and biggest fan in your heart, but who is the guy going to notice the most? Will it be you, in your T-shirt emblazoned with 'Cowboy's Biggest Fan' up on the back row, or the man in the cowboy outfit and the massive Stetson on the front row, with the flare gun?

Eventually, search engines may be able to check every site as a human would, but that is decades off, and would no doubt require artificial intelligence. Till then, SEO is the only real way to equip yourself with that cowboy get-up and flare gun and so get noticed before your dreams of being chosen as the Cowboys' fan of the day turn to so much dust (or maybe that was just *my* dream...).

So now that we know that we have to do SEO to get noticed by the search engines, we need to understand how this translates into a good user experience.

What's a 'good user experience' to a search engine?'

To answer this question, think about it for yourself a second. When you like a page on a website, what do you do?

In our earlier example, what if, instead of finding that junk 'best cat food recipe' page, you found the best site in the entire world for cat food recipes? What would you do? You'd probably bookmark the site, stay there a while, copy some recipes, watch any videos they have and share the website URL on Facebook with all your friends on 'Cat Lover's Anonymous' and that forum at *Cats Forever* magazine.

All of these things show a *very good* user experience. That's what the search engines are looking for from your site and from every page on it. They (the search engines) want your users to have a good user experience with your content, but you won't get many users (in the thousands) unless they can find you and know you exist. This is where SEO comes into its own.

Let's take a moment and focus on you and your business, with this in mind.

What's *your* good user experience?

Now that we know that we need to show the search engines a good user experience, let's consider exactly what that means for you. It depends on what you are trying to accomplish for your website overall and on each of its pages.

- Do you want readers to see your blog?
- Do you want people to buy products from your e-commerce store?
- Are you trying to increase brand awareness for your company?
- Do you want to build an email list of prospects?
- Are you aiming to get leads for your business?
- Are you promoting a cause and requesting donations?

In all the cases above, you require a response from your visitors. This means that each of your web pages needs to be making that action easy for them – even provoking them to make that choice.

If you have an e-commerce store and you SEO it to within an inch of its life but none of your visitors ever buys, what good is it, really? If you create a blog, what would be its point if no one ever looked at it for longer than a few seconds?

The search engines use 'time on site' data as part of their ranking formulas. They look at things such as bounce rate (the percentage rate of users who stay for a few seconds, then return to their search results), how many pages the average visitor goes through, and so on.

If you ignore this factor, you may see your search engine rankings drop over time or, at the very least, watch your competition overtake you in the rankings if they have taken care of it. There is more on this later in the week.

So now is the time to sit back and think like a visitor who has never been to your site before.

- What would *you* want to see?
- What is most important to you as a user?

This is not necessarily what actually *is* most important but what the user *thinks* is most important for them.

- What sort of graphics do you want?

For instance, if you are targeting professors who probably don't want fancy graphics, you probably shouldn't go for a super whiz-bang animated masterpiece but should choose a more refined, academic style.

SUNDAY

MONDAY

TUESDAY

WEDNESDAY

THURSDAY

FRIDAY

SATURDAY

You are most likely an expert in what you are trying to promote but, because sometimes it's hard to take a step back, it might be important for you to ask your friends and family. Be sure to get as much feedback as possible from people who are interested in your topic but not experts in it. Discussion forums and Facebook groups are great places to help you get started and give you comments on your efforts.

Researching your competition

Once you know what you want to do and have an idea of what your visitors want, it's time to do a little initial competitive research. (For more advanced methods of doing this, see Thursday's chapter.)

Let's say you have – or want to set up – a website for your insurance company and you want to see what your competition is and how they're marketing themselves.

1 Pick one of your offerings at random, like home insurance. Go to Google and type it in. If you service a certain geographical area, type in 'home insurance your city'.
2 Now look at how many different results you get. For 'home insurance hoboken' (without the quotation marks), I got about 1,570,000 results.

To narrow down your search, type the search term in quotation marks. For 'home insurance hoboken' I get just 26,000 results. This is because the search engines are showing pages focused on those words in that exact order, which is a better indication of your level of competition for that search term.

3 Take a look at those in the top ten. These ten get about 70 per cent or more of the clicks, depending on the subject and how well it is covered.
4 Click each link and look at what they are doing with their page.
  - Are they focused on getting people signed up to a newsletter?
  - Do they have plenty of content?
  - Do they have a super-slick design or are they minimal in style?
  - Do they give away freebies in exchange for an email address? If so, sign up using a non-work-related email address and see what they do. Keep copies of all emails they send, to give you more ideas.
5 How is the website set up as a whole?
  - Is it a glorified brochure or do they have a tiered website structure with a home page linking to secondary pages?
  - Does there seem to be a constant stream of new information, or is it more static and never changing?
  - Is it a Facebook fan page?

Don't be put off by what looks like a huge SEO mountain to climb when you first type in a search term, as this isn't a true indication of your competition. In reality, the number of your competitors is far, far lower.

Now that you know what the competition is doing, what can you do to improve on what they are doing? How can you make your site more interactive? You know that the search engines love user feedback, so think of how you can offer more ways for users to give you feedback. Be creative here: there are hundreds of online interactions you can create, so make a note always to be thinking of more.

The landscape of the Internet today

Who holds the keys to search right now? Pretty much the universal answer to that question is Google. The sheer massiveness of Google is mind-boggling. According to the latest statistics, Google has roughly 66 per cent of the search market in the US. Yahoo and Bing (Microsoft), which have to some extent now joined forces, have a combined share of around 28–9 per cent. Google is therefore twice as big as the two next largest competitors combined.

For international searches, this number is even larger. In the UK, for instance, Google has a market share of over 90 per cent, with all the other search engines scrabbling around for the scraps. If you are targeting just customers in your own country, it might be worth a quick check to see what Google's market share is where you are.

Google owns not only 'regular search' but also 'video search' (they own YouTube, the third most searched site in the world) and 'image search'. They also dominate 'map search' and looking for local businesses. If you look for it online, Google probably has you covered. This is therefore where you should focus your SEO efforts.

While focusing on optimizing your site for Google, make sure you are also indexed by Bing and Yahoo. Making your site more Google compliant will make your site more Bing compliant, because both are really just looking for the same thing and, with Bing serving up the search results for Yahoo as well as themselves, it cuts down your workload even more.

Summary

Today you learned that SEO does not have to be a mysterious code or formula. It's the key to generating traffic to your site – but not just any traffic: the point of your website is to attract buyers, not just visitors. You have learned what the search engines *really* want – a good user experience – and why you need to SEO. Everything you do should be geared around those two things. If it doesn't make people click or can distract buyers from buying, it should be immediately removed from your site.

We discussed ways to start to research the competition and find out how your competitors attract users to their site. Always do this before you invest in a keyword, to make sure that you can improve on what the competition offers and that you are not wasting your time.

You also learned about the layout of the web as it stands now and why you need to spend your time focusing on optimizing your site for Google.

SUNDAY

MONDAY

TUESDAY

WEDNESDAY

THURSDAY

FRIDAY

SATURDAY

Fact-check [answers at the back]

1. What does SEO stand for?
a) Sequenced echo optimization ❑
b) Search engine orchestra ❑
c) Search engine optimization ❑
d) Sending extras out ❑

2. What's the purpose of SEO?
a) To get a constant stream of visitors to your site ❑
b) To make your pages profitable ❑
c) To get your pages scanned ❑
d) To get your pages noticed by the search engines ❑

3. What do search engines aim to make their search algorithms?
a) As simple as 1-2-3 ❑
b) Harder to crack than the National Security Agency (NSA) mainframe ❑
c) Impossible to analyse completely ❑
d) Open source to everyone ❑

4. How often do search engines change their criteria?
a) Constantly and randomly ❑
b) Every once in a while ❑
c) Every other week ❑
d) Every year ❑

5. What do search engines want the most?
a) Lots of graphics on your site ❑
b) You to be seen by millions ❑
c) A good user experience for their searchers ❑
d) Sites full of advertising ❑

6. If you put a search in quotation marks, what does this make the search engine do?
a) Look for those exact same words in that same order ❑
b) Think you are being sarcastic ❑
c) Do a search for something random ❑
d) Turn on special SEO powers ❑

7. Which of the following can be a website for an online business?
a) A blog ❑
b) A static site ❑
c) A Facebook fan page ❑
d) All of the above ❑

8. How much of everything search-related does Google own?
a) 30 per cent of searches ❑
b) 40 per cent of all traffic ❑
c) 50 per cent of the search engine market ❑
d) Over 65 per cent of everything search-related in the world ❑

9. Who owns YouTube, the third most searched site in the world?
a) Google ❑
b) Yahoo ❑
c) Bing ❑
d) None of the above ❑

10. What percentage of your valuable search engine friendliness time should you spend with Google?
a) 50 per cent ❑
b) 90 per cent ❑
c) 70 per cent ❑
d) 100 per cent ❑

SUNDAY

MONDAY

TUESDAY

WEDNESDAY

THURSDAY

FRIDAY

SATURDAY

MONDAY

Keyword research

Today we will cover the R part of R & D (research and development) for your website. This should always be your first step before you start building any website or web business online, because here is where a business lives or dies. If you already have a website and haven't done this step, it's still possible to do the research and make changes – nothing is carved in stone.

The first part of the research stage involves looking at which keywords (searches) you want to show up for in the search engines/Google. If you don't have traffic, your business dies but – more than that – if you don't get the right *kind* of traffic, your business will also die.

Today you will discover:

- how and where to find out what your potential clients and customers are already searching for
- how to be sure you can get that click from the related search engine results
- what you can do about it if you can't.

What is a keyword?

Keywords are what your potential clients, customers and viewers type into a search engine to get to your site. To take our example from yesterday, 'best cat food recipe' are the four words that comprise the keyword that the user typed in.

The user may have found the same site after typing in simply 'cat food recipe', 'cat food' or even (though extremely unlikely) 'cat' or 'food recipe'. All these phrases are *separate* keywords. Each one has different and various amounts of competition and a varying number of people who type it in.

For short, I am going to call this the *supply and demand* of the keyword. *Supply* is the amount and power of the competition and *demand* is how many people are looking for it. The supply for 'food recipe' is huge, probably in the tens of millions, as is the word 'cat', because there are untold millions of websites that compete for those words. But would you want to rank for those keywords, even if you could?

Why are keywords important?

In our example, we wrote about the 'best cat food recipe' so, if someone were looking for a 'food recipe', they would be unlikely to read your page and they would be gone in a millisecond. Similarly, if they had typed in the keyword 'cat', the same thing would be likely to happen. Neither of these keywords is focused enough; they're just too broad. The person typing in 'cat' may have just wanted the literal definition of the animal, not your amazing one-in-a-million cat food recipe.

One of the simple truths of SEO is that, generally speaking, the more focused the keyword, the better the quality of visitor you'll receive because they are more targeted. However, you need to bear in mind that the more focused the keyword, generally the lower the number of searches that will be performed each month compared to the broader keywords like 'food recipe' or 'home insurance'.

This means that, if you want large numbers of quality visitors coming to your website every day, you will need to create lots of pages, each targeting one of these highly focused keywords (known in the trade as 'long-tail' keywords).

> ## Long-tail keywords
>
> The term 'long tail' was adapted from an article (and later a book) written by *Wired* magazine's former editor-in-chief Chris Anderson, where he discussed the shift in business away from focusing on a relatively small number of one-size-fits-all products, services and customers and instead servicing a potentially much greater number of products and services targeting specific different customers and niches.
>
> His excellent blog on the subject is here: http://longtail.typepad.com/the_long_tail/about.html
>
> It hasn't been updated for a while but is still worth reading.

Applying this principle to your keywords means that, instead of trying to compete with millions of other websites for highly competitive keywords, you create a large number of long-tail keywords that are very specific. Each one will give you a smaller number of searches but, taken as a group, they can give you substantial traffic. Long-tail keyword searches now make up around 70 per cent of all keywords entered into Google and the other search engines. There will be more on reading the mind of your clients through their keywords later today.

Once you know what a keyword is and the types of keywords you need to be focusing on, it's time to dive into creating your own keywords list so that you know which searches you want to show up for.

Generating your initial keyword list

Fortunately for you, Google has provided a free tool that shows you *exactly* the terms people are entering into its search engine and how many approximate searches there are a month. Google's keyword tool is at: https://adwords.google.com/o/KeywordTool

We're going to use your existing website to generate your 'seed' keyword list. If you don't already have a website, pick one of your direct competitors' websites and perform the steps below with it, then repeat the steps for the rest of them.

1 First, take a sheet of paper and across the top write the following headings: **Keyword; Monthly Searches; Competition**.
2 Go to the Google keyword tool and enter your website address – or that of your first competitor – into the website text field in the Find Keywords section. Try it first as domain. com or, if you don't get any results, try www.domain.com
3 For match types, I would deselect 'Broad' and select 'Exact'. Ignore the 'Word or phrase' and 'Category' fields. Leave the 'Only show ideas...' option unchecked. Select the appropriate Advanced options and filters for your chosen language and location.

TIP

It's usually best to leave the defaults on-screen, maybe deleting the country option to give worldwide keyword results. Obviously, if you're only targeting a specific country, make sure you select that country.

4 A short time after you've pressed the Search button you should see a list of keywords that Google believes are relevant to your website.

If you already have a Google AdWords account and are logged in, it will return up to 800 keywords at a time. If you don't have an account, you will receive only 100 keywords per search, but that's plenty to get you started. By the time you have finished this book, you should have a Google AdWords account.

1 Now click the top column heading for *Local Monthly Searches* once, to order it by largest number at the top descending down the page to the smallest number. (If you're targeting a worldwide market, use the *Global Monthly Searches* figures instead.)
2 Now write down all the keywords that are directly relevant to your business and the related number of *Global* or *Local Monthly Searches*.
3 When you're done, take the first keyword, feed it back into Google's keyword tool and generate another list and repeat the procedure. Order the keywords according to *Global* or *Local Monthly Searches* and add any new relevant keywords and their related searches to your list.
4 Repeat this until you run out of keywords to add to your list and then move to the second keyword from your original list, and so on.
5 Next, you take the first keyword and enter it into Google as a regular search within quotation marks (' ') and then note down the number of results Google returns underneath *Competition* on your sheets.
6 Repeat this task for all your keywords. The process may take a few hours, but it is a very important step and shouldn't be ignored. It might be a good idea to assign this task to a staff member if you have someone available.

Once you have the results for your keywords, first you need to decide which of those keywords will be your *primary* keyword. This is the keyword you most want to rank in the search engines for. This keyword will probably have significantly more 'exact match' monthly searches than other keywords and will be difficult to rank for in the beginning but, as you build up your content over time, so you should slowly climb up through the rankings for your primary keyword.

In addition to your primary keyword, you should look at starting with around 50–100 long-tail secondary keywords.

Each secondary keyword should have fewer than 50,000 results back from a 'keyword in quotation marks' search. The number of monthly searches for your primary and secondary keywords will depend on your sector and how competitive it is. Use your judgement with the results and keywords for your niche or industry.

These keywords may be based around your particular market or niche or they could be product names or variations on your theme. If your website is for a service business, it's possible that you may not be able to generate that many relevant keywords, so just generate as many as you can.

If you are targeting a local geographical area, you can append your keywords with your location. For example, instead of trying to rank for 'plumbing supplies', you try to rank for terms like 'plumbing supplies Hoboken NJ'.

If you have or want to build an e-commerce webstore, pay particular attention to keywords that look like 'buying keywords'. These may contain words like 'best' or 'cheapest' or 'review', either at the start or the end. For instance, I once heard of someone who had good success adding the words 'in bulk' to his product keywords. He had an Omega 3 supplement for sale and simply targeted keywords like 'Omega 3 supplements in bulk' and ended up getting quite a bit of targeted traffic.

TIP *When using Google's keyword tool, pay attention to how much it costs to buy ads for the keywords you're going after. This will give you even more insight into how much value your website could have.*

If a keyword has a fairly high comparative search volume per month but the average cost per click (CPC) is quite low, it *could* mean that other businesses haven't had much success in converting searchers into paying customers or clients. On the other hand, if a keyword's CPC is high and its search volume is low, it should mean that – even though it doesn't generate a lot of traffic on its own – because advertisers are willing to pay good money to buy an ad for that keyword, they *could* be converting visitors who click those ads into customers.

Obviously, we don't know for certain whether either of these ideas is true; we can only guess, using a little logical thinking.

The above technique also works well for information sites because, if you decide to place Google AdSense ads on your pages, this can give you an idea of how much the ads hosted on your pages will pay you.

Competitive ranking analysis

Once you have your initial keyword list, you need to whittle it down to the keywords you think you can rank in the top ten results for each of your keywords. The only way to do this is to analyse each of the top ten URLs ranked by Google for each of your keywords.

Since having to go through and examine the top ten URLs for 50–100 keywords would take a very long time, software is available that will automate this task for you while you get on with other activities (see below), but you need to know what information to look for and use some free tools to help give you that data.

It's estimated that more than 200 factors influence how Google ranks URLs for searches, and these are grouped into **on-page** and **off-page factors**. We cover both types in more detail over the next couple of days but, in a nutshell, to increase your chances of ranking:

● 'On-page' factors are the things you can do to your own pages.
● 'Off-page' factors are the things you can do to increase the quality and/or quantity of links pointing to your pages (known as backlinks).

For competitive research purposes, you need to focus on the following factors.

What's the PageRank for the URL in the search results?

PageRank is how Google determines the 'authority' of a specific URL (not just a home page) in its search engine. PageRank is displayed as a numbered scale between 0 and 10, with 10 being given to the most trusted and authoritative sites and pages. This is commonly displayed as PRx, where x is the number.

For example, the BBC News Technology home page has a PageRank of 8 (PR8), which is very, very high because it is deemed by Google to be an 'authority' on the subject of technology. Any content directly or indirectly linked to from that page will eventually inherit some of that PR8 and so that page over time will also gain a certain amount of authority.

Think of a link from a high-PR web page to yours as a 'vote of confidence' on the quality of your content. The more votes of confidence you get from high-authority websites, the more authority *your* pages will get over time and they will eventually rank higher in the results for your keyword.

PageRank used to be the primary factor to ranking high in Google but, after years of being abused by webspammers, Google has downgraded its power. However, in the long term it is still important that you naturally build links from high-PR websites to your site.

How old is the domain name?

Google confers some ranking 'weight' to domains that are older, as they deem them to have more authority in view of their age, assuming they have content on them. Generally, if there are few older domains ranking for your keyword, you'll need to do a little extra work building more quality (i.e. high-PR) links to your pages to counteract the difference in domain age.

How many links point to the URL and the home page?

If a domain's home page has 'authority' due to a decent PR level and/or many links pointing to it but the page that is ranking for your chosen keyword doesn't have either, then it is almost certainly relying on the 'authority' of the domain as a whole. This means that you might have a chance of outranking it, simply by having more good-quality links than it does. This can sometimes explain why some pages from authority sites like Amazon and Wikipedia rank at the top of search results, even though they have few or no backlinks pointing to them.

Do the page's meta title and meta description contain the keyword?

When we talk about the page's title in SEO terms, we mean the <TITLE></TITLE> HTML meta-tag markup, which you see in the very top of your browser window when you visit a web page. This is also the blue underlined text you click on in each of the items in a search results page.

Google likes to see the keyword in the ranking page's title tag, so include it as close to the beginning of your title as possible, but make sure it reads naturally. Don't just throw it in there or try to stuff your <TITLE> with keywords, as Google has a habit of rewriting them to show something completely different.

Advice from Google

Here's a direct quote from a Google employee:

'In general, when we run across titles that appear to be sub-optimal, we may choose to rewrite them in the search results. This could happen when the titles are particularly short, shared across large parts of your site or appear to be mostly a collection of keywords.

'One thing you can do to help prevent this is to make sure that your titles and descriptions are relevant, unique and compelling, without being "stuffed" with too much boilerplate text across your site.'

'JohnMu' Google Webmaster Support Group
(http://bit.ly/X1zDFu)

TIP *Use unique, compelling titles and descriptions on each page of your website.*

25

Does the domain contain the keyword?

If you haven't built your website yet or you're planning to build several external websites pointing to your main 'hub', you'll need to consider whether to have the keyword in the domain name of your new website.

One tactic commonly used until fairly recently was to build a site with a domain name that contained the actual keyword in it. For example, if you want to rank for the search term 'underwater cat juggling' and you have underwatercatjuggling.com as your domain name, you'll get extra credit from Google for having the keyword in the domain name, known as an 'exact match' domain (EMD).

However, after Google rolled out a major update in September 2012 to 'reduce low-quality "exact match" domains from showing up highly in the search results', many sites' rankings fell through the floor. The update was supposed to target low-quality 'spammy' sites built just to show advertising and not much in the way of decent content, but plenty of high-quality sites also seemed to be penalized. This means that having the keyword in your domain name is a less useful tactic than it was.

If you're just starting out and are new to SEO, don't concern yourself with EMDs. Stick to building your brand and, instead of using an EMD, put the keyword in as the page's filename, as in: http://yourdomain.com/underwater-cat-juggling

Is the keyword in any of the HTML headline tags?

Google uses headline HTML tags (H1, H2, H3, H4, H5, H6) to determine what subjects are covered in which sections of the web page.

1 Only use the H1 element once per web page. That should contain the main keyword, so make it the page's content title.
2 Use H2 elements to break the page into different sections, possibly using secondary or related keywords where

they read naturally. Depending on how long your page's content is, you probably won't need more than three or four H2 tags.

3 There are no limits to the number of H2–H6 tags you can use per page, but don't try to keyword stuff them – Google will know and you will feel their wrath.

4 There is usually no need to use H4–H6 tags; H1–H3 are all you should need.

How to get all this information

You can get some data from the free SEOQuake Browser plug-in for Google Chrome and Firefox (seoquake.com), from a free account at opensiteexplorer.org and by checking individual pages.

However, if you don't have time to do all this work or an employee you can assign it to, you can use specialist research software that will semi- or fully automate these tasks while you get on with other things. These keyword and competition research tools are:

- Market Samurai (http://marketsamurai.com)
- Open Site Explorer: shows backlink numbers to individual pages and root domains (opensiteexplorer.org)
- SEOMoz (http://seomoz.org)
- KeywordBlaze (http://keywordblaze.com)

We discuss these software tools and services in more detail on Saturday.

Reading your prospects' minds

At this point, you should be the expert on your niche and passionate about it, and you should know what words your customers are looking for. But do you know what they really want?

You'll remember that you don't want to rank for the keyword 'cat' if you are selling 'cat food' and that we need to think about a good customer experience. This is what comes into play here. For example, the visitor who types in 'Omega 3 in bulk'

SUNDAY

MONDAY

TUESDAY

WEDNESDAY

THURSDAY

FRIDAY

SATURDAY

may be someone who is not just looking for a great deal when buying in bulk but a potential distributor of your product or a store owner who wants to buy your product for their physical store.

As you go through your list of keywords, apply your knowledge of your offering and ask yourself the question, 'What does the person want who types this in?' If it helps, answer that question right next to the main keywords you have chosen with a clear sentence or two. Even if you choose not to do this research stage yourself and prefer to outsource it to a staff member or a third-party outsourcer on odesk.com or elance.com, at least you'll know what needs to be done.

> *An advanced technique you might use to get better at ESP is to run a survey on your site or Facebook page. Actually asking your customers what they want and think might produce some surprising answers.*

Summary

Today you learned how to get started with keyword research by brainstorming and then how to find your niche – what your website will be about – by seeing how much interest it generates. Keep up on this on a monthly basis while always keeping to your core strategy – for example, don't change course to cat supplies if you started at dog supplies.

Even if your keywords start looking better, you will lose time and credibility in Google's eyes if you change your site too much. If you have the time and money, just start a new site and outsource, if you find a good opportunity.

You also discovered the magic of long-tail keywords and how they can help you win more visitors and potential customers. You never really know when these will show up, so make sure that they are actually searched for in some fashion before optimizing for them.

You also started to become an ESP specialist, seeing what your potential clients are looking for when they type in what they do.

SUNDAY MONDAY TUESDAY WEDNESDAY THURSDAY FRIDAY SATURDAY

Fact-check [answers at the back]

1. What are keywords?
a) Curiously shaped letters used to open locks ❏
b) What a customer types in a search engine to find your site ❏
c) Islands in the south of Florida ❏
d) Words with power ❏

2. What does brainstorming help you do?
a) Find what you are an expert at ❏
b) Fine-tune your keywords ❏
c) Learn more about your niche ❏
d) All of the above ❏

3. What are two free tools for SEO work?
a) AdWords keyword tool and SEOQuake ❏
b) KeywordBlaze and SEO Fox ❏
c) SEO Toolbox and Keywords for You ❏
d) Market Samurai and SEOMoz ❏

4. How should you describe the keyword research process?
a) Quick and easy ❏
b) Fun and fast ❏
c) Slow but rewarding ❏
d) A good way to spend Friday night ❏

5. What does a 'niche' mean?
a) A treasure ❏
b) Your area of expertise and profitability ❏
c) A static web page ❏
d) The area of your website set aside for ads ❏

6. What does finding your keyword niche depend on?
a) Your style ❏
b) Your vision for your site ❏
c) What you want to talk about ❏
d) Finding enough interest and keywords that match your area of expertise ❏

7. What are long-tail keywords?
a) High-demand short-length keywords ❏
b) Low-demand and long-length keywords that contain a high-demand keyword ❏
c) High-demand but long-length keywords ❏
d) Low-supply and low-demand keywords ❏

8. Which of these are good words to use in buyer keywords?
a) Best; in bulk ❏
b) World; new ❏
c) Style; amazing ❏
d) Class; series ❏

9. How can you put a possible value on your efforts for an information site?
a) By reading about your niche ❏
b) By watching the news and seeing interest in your niche ❏
c) By using the AdWords keyword tool ❏
d) By signing up for a Google account and looking at the estimated costs of buying keywords that you will rank for ❏

10. What does reading your
    customers' thoughts mean?
a) Having a form of ESP ❏
b) Running a survey ❏
c) Reading about your niche ❏
d) Studying the keywords that
   will find you and asking
   yourself what users want
   when typing them in ❏

TUESDAY

On-page optimization

Many people don't take the time to do any research. They put up a website and expect a constant stream of traffic to magically appear. This *never* happens, so please don't expect it. Instead, think about on-page optimization, which covers what you can do on the pages of the website itself.

You already know how to generate an initial keyword list and how to whittle it down to the keywords that will give you a chance of ranking in the top ten. You even know the software options that can automate this work. Today we'll cover the development part of R & D. This will give you a solid start that many of your competitors won't have and the ability to rank much faster.

You will learn about:

- all the tweaks you can do to the pages on your site to increase your chances of ranking
- your *on-page criteria*; this means that, after you get Google's attention and they look at you, Google knows exactly what you are about.

HTML

Just as with SEO, this four-letter acronym/word may fill you with dread, but the term – just like SEO – doesn't have to be scary.

HTML means HyperText (single word) Markup Language. This is the language that your page is written in. Unless you are building your website from the ground up yourself, this is probably all you really need to know about it. If, like most people, you are using a CMS (content management system) such as WordPress to build your website, putting your content online is no more complicated than making a Word document.

I strongly recommend this CMS option for building a website. After all, you probably couldn't strip your car's engine down and rebuild it – but that doesn't stop you driving it perfectly well. There are probably many thousands of free or low-cost website templates out there for you to find, on wordpress.org among many others. Don't worry about becoming 'cookie cutter' or bland: all of them are pretty flexible and can be customized cheaply by any decent website designer to the point that they become uniquely you.

As you build your site, you will need to consider various elements of SEO, including:

● your home page's title tag
● meta tags and link tags.

Your home page's title tag

The **title** on a web page is the single most important on-page SEO factor. Google uses this piece of information first, to determine the theme of that page and the title on your website's home page, and then to determine the overall theme of your website. So it's pretty important.

If you view the source of a web page, the title tag towards the top of the HTML markup source will look something like this:

```
<HEAD>
<TITLE>example of the title tag for a web page</TITLE>
</HEAD>
```

HOME SWEET MMM

Best practice for the title tag is to use a format like:
    [BRAND/COMPANY] – Primary keyword – Secondary keyword
    or
    Primary keyword – Secondary keyword | [BRAND/COMPANY]
Your home page should contain your primary keyword (the keyword you most want to rank for out of all of your keywords – normally the one with the highest number of searches) and one of your secondary keywords. For interior content web pages, the primary keyword should be the keyword the page's topic is focused on and a naturally occurring secondary keyword.

If you have an e-commerce store with a lot of products for sale or you're a service provider offering many different categories of service, then you could also create a 'landing page' for each category to help direct people to the appropriate product or service they might be looking for.

For example, if you had an e-commerce store selling dog-grooming supplies, you might have the following categories:

- Dog brushes
- Puppy brushes
- Dog scissors
- Dog shampoos

Each of these terms would be the primary keyword for the category landing page, which might have a title like 'Dog shampoos | cleenadogg.com'.

You could show your expertise and optimize the customer's experience even more by having some content about the different types of dog shampoo available and the good and bad points to look out for. Then you might break down your categories even further:

- Organic dog shampoos | cleenadogg.com
- Dog shampoos for long-haired dogs | cleenadogg.com
- Dog shampoos for short-haired dogs | cleenadogg.com

You may have some ideas about how to structure your website from the keyword research you did yesterday. Were there any obvious search queries that might give you ideas for content pages? For example, if there were a lot of searches each month for 'organic dog shampoo', it might be worth putting together a category or sub-category page on the subject. The same goes for service providers; structure your website into categories with relevant and unique title tags and content for each page.

TIP *Remember to keep your TITLE tags to less than 70 characters, as that's the maximum Google will display in their results.*

Why add a blog?

In addition to organizing all your static (mainly never-changing) content and pages on your website, almost all websites can benefit from the installation of a blog. Your blog is where you post your latest news, information, pages, new products, reviews, demonstrations, thoughts related to your business, etc.

Blogs started out as a way for people to write an online journal but they are now a core strategy in e-commerce, to show Google and the other search engines that you have an active and dynamic website and that they need to keep coming back to check for the latest information you've posted.

Everybody wins when you have a constantly updating blog on your site:

● The customer wins because they become more educated and informed about the products and services they might need.

● The search engines win because they are filled with up-to-the-minute information to show people who are searching for it (as well as making money when people click the ads to the right of your 'free' organic results).

● You, the business owner, win because you have more content indexed by the search engines, increasing the chance of someone visiting your website and eventually becoming a customer or client.

HTML meta and link tags

Other HTML elements we can tweak to improve your on-page ranking factors are meta tags and link tags for each page and category. The meta-tags section contains entries like the meta description and meta keywords. This isn't very complicated as Google only really pays attention to a few of these tags, as detailed below.

Meta description

Google pays attention to this as, most of the time when Google scans a web page to be included in its index database, if there is a meta description tag in the HTML source, they will use it as the description that shows up in the search results underneath the page title.

Every web page should have a unique meta description that contains your page's primary keyword as close to the beginning as possible (while still sounding natural) and it also has to try to encourage the searcher to click through to your page – all in 160 characters or fewer (the maximum Google will display).

An example would be:

<META NAME="DESCRIPTION" CONTENT='Looking for an organic dog shampoo that doesn't contain any harmful parabens? Click to see the top five here...'>

(You can ignore the META KEYWORDS tag as Google, Yahoo and Bing don't use it.)

Meta robots

These 'meta robot' tags allow you to specify which individual pages you want the search engine 'bots' (or 'spiders') to index and follow links from and which links and pages to ignore. Not all search engines abide by these tags, but Google, Yahoo and Bing do, as do most reputable smaller search engines.

Like the other meta tags, the robots tag goes between your <head> and </head> markup code.

The commands you can use are:

● "INDEX" (you may index this web page in your search engine)
● "FOLLOW" (you may follow any of the links on this web page)
● "NOINDEX" (do not index this web page)
● "NOFOLLOW" (do not follow any of the links on this web page).

(Google will index and follow links on a web page by default so, strictly speaking, there's no need to use the INDEX and FOLLOW commands.)

You can combine these tags as follows:

<META NAME="ROBOTS" CONTENT="NOINDEX,NOFOLLOW">

This translates to 'Do not index this web page or follow any of the links on this page.'

If you want Google to obey specific commands, change the META name from ROBOTS to GOOGLEBOT, so Google-only commands would be written as:

<META NAME="GOOGLEBOT" CONTENT="NOINDEX,NOFOLLOW">

Additional Google-only commands you can specify with META "GOOGLEBOT" are:

● "NOARCHIVE" (you may not create a cached copy of this page to be accessible from the search results)
● "NOSNIPPET" (do not display a description below the page in the search results and also do not cache a copy of the page)
● "NOODP" This blocks Google from looking for any available description of the page from the Open Directory Project (http://dmoz.org) and using it in their search results.
● "NONE" This is the same as "NOINDEX,NOFOLLOW".

Duplicate content and canonical link elements

One of the biggest SEO no-nos, especially for Google, is 'duplicate content'. Most people who deal with SEO think of duplicate content as two copies of the same web page on the same website, but actually this isn't the case.

For a 'bot', a web page is any unique URL it happens to come across, so potentially these two pages:

● http://underwatercatjuggling.com/siamesesnorkelling.html
● http://underwatercatjuggling.com/siamesesnorkelling.html?affiliate=fyusfys

are treated as two separate, unique pages on your website, even though they are really the same page, with the latter having an affiliate's promotional tracking code added to the end of it.

However, before Google's major Panda update of 2011, Google would just dump what it deemed to be a piece of duplicate content on your site into its 'supplemental index', thus, in effect, removing any ranking ability or power from that page. Now, post-Panda, duplicate content can have a negative effect on what Google sees as your site's overall 'quality' and 'authority' in the index. If Google thinks it's finding too much duplicate content on your site, you might find other pages on your site also losing ranking or, in extreme circumstances, dropping out of Google's index altogether.

Fortunately, this potentially serious issue is easily remedied by using the link canonical element, which tells Google the canonical – or preferred – URL of the web page added into the <HEAD></HEAD> section of your web page's HTML code: <LINK REL="CANONICAL" HREF="http://www.yourdomain. com/page.html" />

In addition to letting Google know the preferred URL to use for each web page, you also need to let them know your preferred choice of formatting for your domain name – either with or without the 'www' at the beginning. To do this, you need first to sign up for a Google webmaster tools account, if you don't already have one, at:

http://google.com/webmaster/tools

If you already have a Google or Gmail account, log into it and then go to this URL. Once in there, follow the instructions on this page:

http://support.google.com/webmasters/bin/answer. py?hl=en&answer=44231

(Your best bet is to hand this job to your preferred outsourcer.)

Primary keyword in page URL, or permalink

Every page you create needs a unique URL. If you're creating your website using individual HTML web pages, this is the filename of the page – for example, 'siamese-snorkelling.html'.

When you use a content management system like WordPress to create your website content, each page is generated from a combination of content stored in its database while the design of the site is stored in separate 'template' or 'theme' files. Each of these 'pages' has a unique URL called a permalink, which generally doesn't have the file extension '.html' at the end.

So, for example, the Siamese Snorkelling page created in a CMS like WordPress would probably have a URL like http://yourdomain.com/siamese-snorkelling. For SEO purposes, they are the same and you should use the web page's primary keyword as the filename or the permalink.

On-page content

If you don't narrow down your content so that you have clear criteria for each page, Google gets confused and you'll end up ranking poorly or not at all. If you don't want this to happen to you, follow today's guidance to the letter.

You can consider the various elements of your on-page content by asking yourself the following questions about it.

How long should the page be?

The simple answer to this is 'as long as it needs to be'. This may seem to be an evasive answer, but it's true. For example, if you have content on a category landing page for 'organic dog shampoo', the page probably doesn't need to be that long – maybe

400–500 words. If it's more of an article page, talking about 'How to avoid the seven most common mistakes when training your German Shepherd' or sales copy on a product's page on an e-commerce website, then make the length as long as it needs to be to cover everything you want to cover. On the whole, Google likes longer content, provided it's relevant to the page's subject.

What on-page tricks will boost my chances of ranking?

1 **Upload a video to your YouTube channel.**
This should be focused around the same primary keyword as your page and then embedded into the page using the code YouTube gives you. The video could be a demonstration of a product, a spoken version of the text on the page or you talking in more detail about one part of the content.

Google and YouTube

Google *loves* video and especially loves it when you embed video from YouTube. The number of times a video is embedded and the number of views it gets are two of the main ranking factors for the video to show up in YouTube searches, which are separate from Google's main search engines. So you can kill two birds with one stone!

2 **Create an account on Scribd.com and upload PDF documents to it.**
You can embed these or link them to your pages where relevant. The Scribd.com home page has a PageRank of 8, so it's fair to say that Google loves Scribd. Every document has its own page on Scribd, and so your document page will inherit a tiny fraction of the Scribd PageRank after it's trickled down through the website, so it might also end up ranking for your primary or secondary keywords, depending on how competitive they are.

PDFs could be usage and configuration instructions for a product, a partial transcript of the video on your page with a link to the page at the end, recipes with your product as the star, tips and tricks and so on.

What should the keyword density be?

This is the number of times a keyword is mentioned on a web page, expressed as a percentage of total word count. If you had 1,000 words on a web page and your keyword was used 10 times, your keyword density would be 1 per cent.

Google Penguin – an overview

Google's Penguin update of April 2012 was designed to reward high-quality sites and to 'punish' those using low-quality SEO techniques (like keyword stuffing) to artificially rank higher than they deserved to. In Google's own words:

'In the pursuit of higher rankings or traffic, a few sites use techniques that don't benefit users, where the intent is to look for shortcuts or loopholes that would rank pages higher than they deserve to be ranked. We see all sorts of webspam techniques every day, from keyword stuffing to link schemes that attempt to propel sites higher in rankings.'

Matt Cutts, Google Webmaster Central Blog
(http://bit.ly/12l8Jx2)

Penguin was designed to combat over-optimization of a web page, e.g. by aggressively including the page's primary keyword too many times or getting too many backlinks pointing to the page with targeted keywords as the anchor text (the actual text containing the link).

Years ago, you could rank highly in Google just by adding dozens of keywords to the bottom of each web page, changing the font and colours so they were invisible or virtually invisible to the visitor. Do not even think about trying to do this. It hasn't been advisable to use this technique for several years now, but since Google's Penguin update of 2012 it has been almost suicide to try it.

Although Google doesn't specifically track and monitor the keyword density on a web page, they do track and monitor other related factors. What's important is that you use your keywords naturally (for the users) and you don't use them too often (for both the users and the search engines).

How much is too much? Lots of opinions are out there; I recommend erring on the low side and staying under 2 per cent. Follow that and also bear in mind that, if you read through your page and you feel that it might be too much, the engines will probably feel the same.

What about headline tags (the H1–H6 tags)?

As discussed yesterday when we were researching your competition, these HTML heading tags are what the engines look for to see what is most important in a page's content (you can find these in the heading section of any legitimate CMS). H1 defines the most important heading, while H6 defines the least important.

- **H1** is only for the title right at the top of the page and will contain your main keyword. (You can probably just use the page title again.)
- **H2** is for your main sub-categories on the page. One should contain your main keyword and the others should contain the other naturally related keywords. This is not a hard-and-fast rule, though; only do it if it flows naturally.
- **H3** should be only for subheadings under H2 tags or for other points of interest, links, etc. It should be used sparingly.

These three are easy to add to your pages and, because they create your pages' structure, they help search engines categorize your pages more efficiently, which helps improve your rankings. To keep things simple, you don't need to use the H4–H6 tags; it can get a little confusing if you do try to use them.

What about images and videos?

Use these wherever possible. They will give you extra points, especially the images, because you can even get extra traffic from them in Google and Yahoo.

Rules for images

● Your image should have the name of what it is. It's not helpful to have a name like DSC-394908, which is no use to Google. So you should name it properly as, say, 'Dog-hair-clippers.jpg' or, better still, 'dog-hair-clippers-for-long-haired-dogs.jpg'. This can sneak in your long-tail keyword where only the search engine notices it, and keep it 'legal'.

● Add an 'ALT' tag that has the same text as the filename. An 'ALT' tag is written like this in HTML:

```
<IMG src=".../images/dog-hair-clippers-for-long-
haired-dogs.jpg" alt="Dog Hair Clippers For
Long-haired Dogs">
```

Most CMS programs will let you add this in when you add the image. If you have multiple images on a page, do not name or ALT *all* the images with the same keyword – Google classes this as 'webspam' and therefore bad.

Rules for videos

● Make sure it is a YouTube video (Google loves them because they own them).
● On YouTube, it needs to be set to a public video.
● The video title should also contain your long tail as well as the description in the video itself loaded on YouTube.
● Do not make it autoplay; make the user click it to play (user interaction is a ranking factor on YouTube, albeit probably a small one as it is a factor that is potentially easy to 'game').

LSI: is it important?

LSI, or Latent Semantic Indexing, is a process Google uses to discover words and phrases that are related to each other and the context of the document they are in, to help decide whether a page should rank for a particular keyword. Google does this programmatically with specialist software and huge server power.

From your perspective as a website owner, all you need to do is make sure you have additional keywords on the page that are related to the page's primary keyword. For example, the keyword 'broken dentures' might generate the following related keywords using LSI: dentist, tooth, fix, denture repair, cosmetic dentistry, denture repair kit, emergency dentist. You can see that all the words are related to the original term.

Don't worry too much about trying to include a certain number of LSI-related keywords in your page's content. Just add something when it's relevant and when it would naturally appear. Don't try to force a keyword in there just for the sake of it. Be natural and real in your content and you will have no problems with Google. Try to trick them and... well, you already know what happens then...

Technical considerations

It's also important to take into account the following technical considerations when looking at on-page optimization:

- your site loading speed
- your file sizes
- caching
- your IP address.

Maximize your site loading speed

One important ranking factor that few people know about is the time it takes for a web page to load in a browser. Since Google wants the best experience possible for visitors, it cares about this and makes it a direct factor in its ranking formula.

According to an article in the *New York Times* (1 March 2012), research by Google shows that web users tend to be impatient of slow-loading sites. The average time a visitor expects a web page to take to load is within six seconds across the world – but only around 3.5 seconds in the US. People will visit a website less often if it's slower than a competitor's by a quarter of a second! Speed therefore matters, not just for ranking purposes but also to stop visitor abandonment.

The three best ways to optimize your site's loading speed are as follows:

- Make sure you're running on the fastest server possible within your budget.
- Minimize the sizes of web pages, images and other related files on your site.
- Use caching wherever possible, if you are using a CMS or other database-driven website system.

Web hosting is now extremely cheap in comparison with paying shop rents and business rates, so don't penny-pinch. You can get great super-fast hosting from as little as £5 ($8) a month from a simple shared hosting account, right up to £500 ($800) a month for a fully maintained server just for your website.

It can be difficult to determine exactly what level of hosting your website requires, especially when most basic shared hosting packages can come with what looks like more bandwidth resources than you'll ever need. In web-hosting parlance, bandwidth (sometimes called data transfer) is the amount of data in megabytes (or sometimes terabytes) your website can serve to your visitors per month. That's for every web page, every image and every single file on your website.

Even though basic hosting packages can come with quite substantial-looking bandwidth allocations, what they don't cover is the number of visitors they can handle at the same time. I learned this lesson over time when one of my websites became extremely popular, to the point where today it attracts nearly 1,000 visitors an hour, every hour. I had to upgrade my server's power rapidly to stop it from gradually slowing down, and then freezing and having to be rebooted every day.

If this had kept happening every time Google came back to scan my site, I would almost certainly have lost some of my hard-earned rankings and income.

Minimize your file sizes

Likewise, do whatever you can to minimize the sizes of all the files on your site, particularly images. Be aware that simply resizing a large image down so it's smaller on the page doesn't make it any quicker to load. If you've got high-quality images, get an in-house graphic person (or external outsourcer) to run them through Photoshop and create web-friendly versions of them.

By simply using default settings, you can easily reduce large, high-quality image files and resize them down so that they fit nicely on a web page with a final file size that's tiny in comparison to the original, and with barely a noticeable difference in quality. You'll be surprised how much of an increase in speed you can achieve when you optimize everything.

Make sure that your coding meets W3C standards. This is not necessarily a ranking factor but it can help Google index your information that much faster.

You can find a great validation checker here: http://validator.w3.org/

Use caching

Caching works particularly well if you have a database-driven site that generates pages 'on the fly', rather than having a site consisting of static HTML pages. With a database-driven site – for example, one made with a content management system like WordPress – every time a visitor requests to display a certain page, the CMS has to go through all the procedures needed to create that page. So it has to connect with the database, search for the required content, pull the content out, locate the page template and render the completed page.

This all takes time and server resources, which doesn't help you if you have a lot of people visiting your site at the same time and/or an underpowered server. A far better idea is to see if you can set up a static version of your page and display that instead. WordPress can do this, via a free plug-in called W3 Total Cache, and other CMS systems like Joomla give you the option to do this as well.

If you're not sure, speak to your tech person to see if it's possible on your system.

Have a unique IP address

Your IP address is the string of numbers separated by periods that identify a computer on a network, in this case the Internet. On the Internet this becomes slightly more complicated if you have a shared web-hosting account, because there may be many dozens or hundreds of websites that are assigned the same IP address.

Ideally, you should spend a little more per month and get a unique IP address. There are two main reasons why this is a good idea:

1 A website you share an IP address with may be aggressively doing bad SEO. While there's no proof that Google would punish all websites on that IP address, for the sake of a slightly larger monthly outlay you can protect yourself from this possibility.

2 If you're thinking about setting up secure e-commerce facilities directly on your website, you'll need a unique IP address assigned to your website before you purchase your secure certificate.

Content reorganization

We've already talked about the best ways to organize your information on your website. If you have an existing website with a structure that you want to change, you need to make sure you have some search engine redirects in place to tell Google and the other search engines where your new pages are. You can find more information on redirects here: http://www.webconfs.com/how-to-redirect-a-webpage.php

(The main redirect I use is a 301 – a permanent redirect.)

Get your robot director going

This is known as a robots.txt file. This tells the search engine bots where to go and to differentiate the important things from the unimportant. Some CMS programs generate this automatically. To read more about robots.txt files, go here: http://www.robotstxt.org

If your site doesn't have one, or your CMS doesn't generate one, here's a free online robots.txt generator: http://tools.seobook.com/robots-txt/generator/

Send your sitemap to the search engines

After you have built and launched your site, you want to make it as easy as possible for Google and Bing to come and scan all the pages on your website, so you need to create and submit a sitemap to them. (Yahoo no longer has its own algorithm and only uses Bing; it is now pretty much just a news portal with a Bing search box.)

Some content management systems are able automatically to generate a sitemap, either directly or with the use of a plug-in. For WordPress users, I recommend the free WordPress SEO plug-in by Yoast:

http://wordpress.org/extend/plugins/wordpress-seo/

If your website cannot automatically generate its own sitemap, Google has kindly created a free online tool to help you generate a sitemap yourself:

http://code.google.com/p/googlesitemapgenerator/

It will also need to be loaded on your site and refreshed frequently if it is not automated. Google checks your page frequently and that is the first place it goes.

Once you are done, go here to submit it to Google:

http://google.com/webmasters

and then here for Bing:

http://www.bing.com/toolbox/webmaster/

Be sure to update your sitemap every time something changes on your site or, if that's too inconvenient, just do it once every week or two. Don't overdo it: the search engines don't like it and you'll just look like that kid in your year at school who was always desperate for attention – 'Look at me, look at me!'

Summary

Today you learned how to make your pages ready for Google to have a look and, when they look, to like what they see. You now know how to optimize your pages for keywords. Keep your site structure simple (two or three tiers) and remember to put your keywords in everything, from the domain name to the fine print, but without overdoing it.

It cannot be over-emphasized that it's vital to make your site interactive. Embed YouTube videos, good content, places to comment and leave feedback, as well as product review sections and other features all over the place for your customers to enjoy.

Tomorrow we are going to look at off-page ranking factors, which is the next area of SEO to tackle once you are happy with your on-page factors.

SUNDAY

MONDAY

TUESDAY

WEDNESDAY

THURSDAY

FRIDAY

SATURDAY

Fact-check

1. What does HTML stand for?
   a) Hyper Text Management Language ❏
   b) HyperText Markup Language ❏
   c) High Text Meta Links ❏
   d) Human Text Markup Language ❏

2. For domain name SEO, what should you aim to do?
   a) Always think of something cool and unique ❏
   b) Put in some random numbers and letters ❏
   c) Concentrate on branding rather than trying to put keywords in it ❏
   d) Aim to be the next Google ❏

3. Titles on a home page should optimize for no more than how many keywords?
   a) One ❏
   b) Two ❏
   c) Three ❏
   d) Four ❏

4. How many keywords should you optimize all the other titles for?
   a) One ❏
   b) Two ❏
   c) Three ❏
   d) Four ❏

5. Which H tags are not really needed?
   a) H1 ❏
   b) H2 ❏
   c) H3 ❏
   d) H4–6 ❏

6. What kind of keyword should images and videos have?
   a) None – they don't need keywords in them ❏
   b) They should be full of the main keyword ❏
   c) They should be focused on a related long-tail keyword ❏
   d) They should always be random numbers and letters ❏

7. How useful are frames, Flash and hidden keywords?
   a) Fairly useful but not essential ❏
   b) Vital ❏
   c) Only if you have time to do them ❏
   d) A bad idea, always ❏

8. What is LSI?
   a) Probably a red herring ❏
   b) Unimportant ❏
   c) Useless to try and guess ❏
   d) How Google finds related keywords to help decide the topic of a page ❏

9. Why is page load time a ranking factor used by Google?
   a) They want the best experience possible for visitors ❏
   b) People will visit a website less often if it's slower than a competitor's ❏
   c) They want to make it as difficult as possible for you to get into the top ten ❏
   d) They want you to spend more money on your server ❏

10. How often should you resubmit your sitemap to Google and Bing?

a) Every day ❑

b) Every time something changes on your site ❑

c) Once a year ❑

d) Never ❑

WEDNESDAY

Off-page optimization

You now know how to build and structure your website to get the maximum SEO benefit from it, so all you need now are visitors. Today, in the second development day of your SEO training, you will learn how to increase the chances of ranking even further, by creating high-quality links that point back to pages on your site.

You've already considered the kinds of things you do when you find a website you like, and now you'll find out how to apply those factors to your own site. It really all comes down to how much people like you and how much they show that love to you, and today we're going to be talking in detail about:

- backlinks and external PageRank, and how to examine and improve your backlink profile
- a major change, called AuthorRank, that will probably alter SEO as we know it and how you can start positioning yourself to take advantage of it now.

Why are backlinks important?

As mentioned on Monday, backlinks are links from a page on someone else's website to a page on your site. They are normally shown as blue, underlined text, although they may be another colour and not underlined. But most webmasters now stick to the de facto standard of blue and underlined.

Images can also be made into hyperlinks that can take you somewhere else when clicked.

Backlinks are important when it comes to SEO because they are at the core of how Google decides to rank individual web pages for keyword-related searches. It measures this using a system called PageRank.

What is PageRank?

As also mentioned on Monday, PageRank is Google's method of determining how trustworthy and authoritative the content is on a page. The more trustworthy Google considers a page to be, the higher it sets its PageRank (PR).

If you get a high-PR web page linking to one of your web pages, some of that PR will be passed on to your web page and Google will – all things being equal – begin to treat it as an authority on your page's topic. It will begin to use that as a possible factor in ranking your page for the primary keyword.

PageRank is just one of more than 200 factors Google uses to determine the ranking of a page for a keyword. Getting high-PR backlinks to your web page on their own is no guarantee that you will ever rank for a keyword, but common sense will tell you that it certainly wouldn't hurt.

It makes sense that Google would see this as a good thing, as high-PR (trusted) links pointing to another page are a 'vote of confidence' that the information on the page in question is good and relevant and something visitors might find useful.

Since getting these high-PR backlinks isn't always easy, some marketers and SEO people started to switch quality for quantity. They would use automated software and cheap outsourcers in India and the Philippines to blast hundreds and thousands of low-quality links (such as blog comments and links in web 2.0 profile pages and discussion forum signatures) and ended up ranking many low-quality sites in Google in the top ten for their keywords.

Google has been on the attack to eliminate these 'webspam' pages from their index, and this culminated in their Penguin update of 2012. The update covered both on-page and off-page webspam behaviour, so you need to know about some off-page tactics that you can use to avoid being caught out.

Penguin and off-page optimization

On 24 April 2012, Google released its webspam update, which eventually became known by Google's internal name of Penguin. Its purpose was to punish people who had aggressively 'over-optimized' their website to rank or, in other words, had been using tactics against Google's webmaster guidelines (which are compulsory reading if you want your website to show up somewhere in Google).

If you already have a website and – after checking your web stats software – noticed a significant drop in site traffic after 24 April, you were hit by Penguin. You weren't alone: Penguin affected approximately 3.1 per cent of all English-speaking Google results.

Find Google's webmaster guidelines at:

http://support.google.com/webmasters/bin/answer. py?hl=en&answer=35769

Examining your backlink profile

As the name suggests, your backlink profile is the overall picture of *all* the backlinks pointing to all the pages on your site.

To generate your backlink profile:

● register for a free account with opensiteexplorer.org
● enter your home-page URL
● click the Search button.

A free account with OSE will give you the first 1,000 backlinks. If you have more than that, sign up for the free 30-day trial of the Pro version and run the search again. When you get the results, filter them by selecting the following from the drop-down menu options above the results:

● Show *all* links from only external pages to pages on this root domain.
● If you have a Pro account, show links ungrouped and click the Filter button.

Now you can download a copy of all your results in CSV format ready for importing into Excel or, if you're more of a visual person (like me), ready for uploading into Link Detective: http://www.linkdetective.com ← *free account available*

Depending on the number of backlinks you have in your CSV file, it might take a little while for Link Detective to process them, but eventually it will generate two graphs: one showing the type of backlinks and the second grouping your links by the anchor text they use, which, if you remember, is just the text that is linked (blue and underlined) on the originating page that's pointing to your page.

There are several things to consider here: link diversity, unnatural anchor text profile, low-quality links, relevant links and link velocity. You also need to look at when to use rel='nofollow' and at other linking no-nos.

Link diversity

Looking at your link-type graph, ideally you should have a large variety of different types of links pointing back to each URL on

SUNDAY

MONDAY

TUESDAY

WEDNESDAY

THURSDAY

FRIDAY

SATURDAY

your site. No one type of link should have a significantly higher percentage than the others, especially with link types Google can class as 'spammy', like (forum) profiles and blog comments.

If you have one or more link types with a percentage that is quite a bit higher, do what you can either to have those links to your site removed or to increase the percentage of your other link types so that they even out across all your links.

Unnatural anchor text profile

While you want a diverse 'footprint' of link types pointing to your website pages, you don't want a large number of links using the same 'anchor text' pointing to your pages. This is one of the main 'over-optimization' factors Google stamped on with their size 11 steel-toecapped boots.

The second Link Detective graph will show you your anchor text profile for the URL you entered in Open Site Explorer. What you're looking for is a fairly even spread of different anchor text wording across all the links.

I personally like to keep each anchor text percentage on the low side, around 6 or 7 per cent, and, while I do use primary and secondary keywords linking to relevant pages, I also use anchor text that doesn't contain any of my keywords. This could be anchor text like:

- [www.mydomain.com]
- [click here]
- [check this out]
- [website]
- [My Company Name]

Examine your CSV file in Excel, or whatever spreadsheet software you use, and sort it by anchor text and then by domain authority.* If you have a batch of anchor text higher than 7 per cent of your total backlinks, you need to contact the websites linking to you and using anchor text that has a domain authority of 20 or less and ask them to remove that link.

> * Domain authority is Open Site Explorer's best guess as to how well (or not) a website will rank in Google's search engine rankings. It is generally seen by the SEO industry as comparable to PageRank.

Link spam (low-quality links)

If you've been doing manual backlink building, the chances are that you won't run into this problem. The most common cause of having large numbers of low-quality links pointing to pages on your site is using automated software or cheap outsourced labour. Using these methods, it's possible to generate hundreds, thousands or even tens of thousands of low-quality links. If that's something you have done in the past, it's unlikely that you'll have the time or resources to remove these links. You therefore need to start manually building high-quality, relevant links from authority sites in your niche or sector, to mitigate the effects of the bad links.

 See this post for 17 different types of link spam to avoid using:

http://www.seomoz.org/blog/17-types-of-link-spam-to-avoid

Link relevance

It's common sense that it's more likely for a site on a certain topic (let's say Harley Davidson motorcycles) to be linked to by other relevant sites (those that talk about Harleys, motorcycles in general, the history of Hell's Angels, etc.). Of course, you do get the odd one or two links that might not seem obvious at first glance (like a link from the owner of an orange grove on his bio to a page that has a picture of his first Harley), but on the whole the vast majority of links pointing to a page should come from pages deemed by Google to be 'on theme' – in other words, related to the subject on the page and the site in general.

We don't know exactly how Google determines relevance, but we can assume that they use a combination of:

● TITLE tag
● H1 and H2 headline HTML tags
● the text surrounding the link if it's in the main page content
● the overall topic of the page.

Your aim is to make sure that most links pointing to each page on your website are related, by content and by subject.

Link velocity

Link velocity is just a fancy way of describing how fast you build links to your web pages.

In the days when Google couldn't index and rank pages at the speed they do now, if they detected large numbers of links suddenly appearing to a fairly new site (less than six months old), they would 'sandbox' the site to the bottom of their index until they determined the validity of the links pointing to the various pages. They would then rank each page accordingly, which could take as long as 18 months.

Getting large numbers of links pointing back to your pages in a comparatively short time *can* be a flag for Google, especially if your website is new. However, the key here is the quality of links you get and the age and PageRank of your website. If your website suddenly gets tens of thousands of low-quality, spam-type links in a short time, then Google, rightly, will smell a rat.

If, on the other hand, your website is mentioned on the news and you suddenly get tens of thousands of links from reputable websites within a short period, the chances are that you won't be penalized. In addition, if your website is well established and has a high PageRank, the less likely it is that you would be flagged as a potential webspammer, should you get a sudden influx of links in a short time.

Rel='nofollow'

'Nofollow' works in the same way as it does for the 'nofollow' instruction in the meta robots tag discussed yesterday, except that rel='nofollow' allows you to specify exactly which links you wish Google to ignore:

<a href='aboutme.html' rel='nofollow'>About Me</a>

When a link is formatted to be nofollow, Google will not index it, follow where it goes or pass any PageRank through to it (as long as no one else is linking to that page without the rel='nofollow' or a link to that page is in a sitemap.)

There are two reasons to 'nofollow' a link:

1 If someone has paid for a text advertisement on your website, it's against Google's webmaster guidelines to buy or sell links that pass PageRank (see Other linking no-nos, below).
2 The content is untrusted. For instance, if you run a popular blog with high PageRank and you get lots of people commenting, you may want to prevent spammers from trying to automate their blog comments in the hope of getting lots of PR power from you without contributing anything useful.

Other linking no-nos

Again, direct from the same page as above from Google, the following are examples of link schemes that can negatively impact a site's ranking in search results:

- **Buying or selling links that pass PageRank** This includes exchanging money for links, or posts that contain links; exchanging goods or services for links; or sending someone a 'free' product in exchange for them writing about it and including a link.
- **Excessive link exchanging** ('Link to me and I'll link to you.')
- **Linking to web spammers** or unrelated sites with the intent to manipulate PageRank
- **Building partner pages** exclusively for the sake of cross-linking
- **Using automated programs** or services to create links to your site

Don't be tempted to do any of this type of linking. You might be lucky and it might work for a while, but eventually your luck will run out and your rankings, and possibly your revenue, will drop.

Case study: A drop in the rankings

In 2011 the website for J. C. Penny, the US retailing giant, was the target of an investigation by the *New York Times*, who were amazed at how well they were doing in Google's rankings. It turned out that the SEO company they'd hired seemed to have used tactics that contravened Google's webmaster's guidelines and, for a short while, the J. C. Penny website was nowhere to be found in Google after 'manual action was taken'.

http://www.nytimes.com/2011/02/13/business/13search.html

Eventually, they were back in Google, but it must have been a frantic, painful time for the management team, not to mention expensive in hiring another, more reputable SEO firm to fix those errors, and it probably did them some branding damage too.

Don't make the same mistake!

AuthorRank: a seismic shift in SEO

Until now, we've discussed PageRank, which Google uses to determine the authority of a page based on the quality and relevance of the links pointing to it. Google has now introduced another measurement of authority, called AuthorRank. Unlike PageRank, which applies a quality value to individual links pointing to a page, AuthorRank monitors the number of times your content is tweeted and retweeted on Twitter, liked and shared on Facebook and generally spread around the social networks. AuthorRank applies the value to *you*, the author.

The more you create unique, high-quality, interesting content and the more this is spread by relevant, authoritative people, the more Google deems you to be an authority in your field, your sector, your niche. And the more authority you have, the more quickly you will move up the ranks in Google's index.

Everything you have learned so far in this book is still important (creating a good user experience, making the user want to share your page, search around, like you and post your page in other places, etc.) but you also need to start telling Google you're an expert in your field as well. To do this, you need to:

- get a Google+ account
- link everything you can to it, including your website and/or blog, and share all your articles, etc.
- make a lot of friends on there and share back and forth as much as possible
- use your Google account to log in everywhere you go, if possible
- make a point of linking everything possible to your name, i.e. sign them always with the same name from your Google+
- use the same photo all the time.

Do all of these steps, and more if you can think of them. Essentially, make it so that Google can track the content you create and see how it does. If you are creating good content, this will turn into a good thing for you because you will be prepared when others aren't.

 For more detail on setting up Google+ as well as all the other major social networks, see my book **Teach Yourself Successful Social Media Marketing In A Week.**

Make the most of AuthorRank

To make the most of AuthorRank, make your content as good as you can and link it to your name and reputation as much as possible. This will give you good AuthorRank and, in time, all this excellent quality content passed around by bigwigs in your industry, sector or niche will link back to your site and – because you did it all under one name – it will definitely be a factor in ranking in the future, sooner rather than later.

AuthorRank also ties into the idea of Google directly monitoring the likes, shares, retweets, etc., that a page gets, so the more of these social signals that are pointing to a URL, the higher the chances are that it will rank, in combination with the other ranking factors.

There's no hard, definitive proof that Google is doing this but, if we apply a little common sense and think about how influential social networks like Facebook, Twitter, LinkedIn, Instagram and Google+ are quickly becoming, it seems very likely.

Here's an excellent blogpost on the subject of social signals and also AuthorRank:

http://www.seomoz.org/blog/your-guide-to-social-signals-for-seo

Go out and get links, but aim for quality not quantity, and don't take short cuts. Do start thinking about AuthorRank and your social 'footprint'.

Summary

Today we have talked about what backlinks are and why they are important for your site. You learned what good and bad links look like, where not to put your links and how to give the user a good experience when they click on that link. A good link is one to another page containing keywords related to your keywords, from a good, high-authority site. YouTube is a great example of where you can make these links yourself.

You have also learned about the significance of AuthorRank and the social signals that arise from your social networks. You now need to start preparing for them both, just to be safe. So get yourself a Google+ account and get active with Facebook – whether you like them or not.

SUNDAY MONDAY TUESDAY WEDNESDAY THURSDAY FRIDAY SATURDAY

Fact-check [answers at the back]

1. What are backlinks?
   a) Connections at the back of your computer ❏
   b) The back pages of your website ❏
   c) Where website codes are stored ❏
   d) Links to your website from other sites ❏

2. How important are backlinks for SEO?
   a) You need lots of backlinks from all over the web to rank in Search ❏
   b) You need only high-quality, relevant backlinks ❏
   c) You need to get as many links as possible as quickly as possible ❏
   d) Only if you use automated programs to get them ❏

3. When it comes to links, what wins over what every time?
   a) Quantity over quality ❏
   b) Quality over quantity ❏
   c) Authority over relevance ❏
   d) Automated programs over fashion ❏

4. How important is it to buy links?
   a) Very important ❏
   b) You should never do it ❏
   c) OK in moderation ❏
   d) Google doesn't care ❏

5. How important is it to get links on a similar page to yours, after asking the owner of the site?
   a) Essential ❏
   b) Bad ❏
   c) Google doesn't care ❏
   d) OK in moderation ❏

6. According to Google, what is your site's ranking in their results based on the analysis of?
   a) The quantity of links pointing to you ❏
   b) The quality of links pointing to you ❏
   c) The speed you acquire the links pointing to you ❏
   d) The relevance of links pointing to you ❏

7. Getting a large number of links very quickly to your site is:
   a) A core part of your SEO strategy ❏
   b) Very bad and never to be attempted ❏
   c) OK, providing that they are quality links from reputable websites and your website has enough age and PageRank ❏
   d) A way to move up the rankings ❏

8. What does rel='nofollow' mean in an HTML hyperlink?
   a) It tells the search engines you don't understand something ❏
   b) Don't follow the link or pass PageRank to the destination ❏
   c) Ignore all the links on the current page ❏
   d) The link is highly trusted ❏

9. How should you make the most of AuthorRank?
a) By making your content as good as you can ❏
b) By using the same photo all the time ❏
c) By writing a blog about it ❏
d) By telling everyone in your address book about it ❏

10. What are the key lessons in off-page optimization?
a) Get quality not quantity links ❏
b) Set up an account on Google+ to take advantage of AuthorRank ❏
c) Creating great content and linking it to your reputation will help make you an authority and probably rank higher in Google in the future ❏
d) All of the above ❏

THURSDAY

Getting other traffic sources to your website

Once you have got your website up and started getting traffic from the search engines, you'll realize that it comes as just a trickle to begin with. However, there are more ways to get traffic to your site beyond mighty Google.

These other tried and tested methods involve using three major sites that you will have heard about; they each deserve a separate book to themselves. These sites are none other than YouTube, Amazon and Facebook. They are all behemoths, up there with Google. YouTube is the third most visited site in the world and, to all intents and purposes, the second biggest search engine (over Bing), Amazon is the largest online retailer and Facebook is the largest and most visited non-search engine site in the world.

Fortunately for us, they cost nothing or very little for you to leverage them. Today you'll learn some basic dos and don'ts and ways to get started.

YouTube

YouTube, the second biggest 'search engine' after Google, is also owned by Google. This means that videos put on YouTube instantly get more Google 'love' than any other video service and often end up in the top ten of Google quickly, with little effort. Putting your link in the video's description will certainly not hurt your SEO efforts either.

Almost any business in the world could benefit from several YouTube videos, so it is worth paying attention and working out how your business could take advantage of this opportunity.

If you have a webstore, you could use YouTube to show:

- videos that feature your products
- how-to videos on your products
- video reviews of products you sell
- your major marketing campaigns
- fun videos featuring your products indirectly.

TIP *If you get a good writer and fun material for your YouTube video, it could well go viral, which would be pure commercial gold for your business.*

If you have an informational niche site, you could post:

- informational videos
- how-to videos surrounding your niche
- interviews with experts in your niche
- testimonials from readers/users.

If you run professional services, you could post:

- interactive videos about your services
- client testimonials
- interviews that you have given to other related businesses.

If you offer local services, you could post:

- videos of your staff, so that customers can 'meet' the person who will come and paint their ceiling or check their drain

- solutions to simple problems to demonstrate your expertise
- videos of local events, featuring your business as an ad at the front.

These are just a few examples of what's possible; the list is endless. You could even simply make a visual or an audio file, or post still pictures of participants and have an interview playing in the background.

Making the most of YouTube

Some videos get a lot of views, but that does not mean they get a lot of people clicking on your site to find out more. To make it more likely that one of your videos is successful, use all the resources you have available, bearing in mind the following top tips.

Make lots of videos

You never know what will go viral and what won't. Certain videos will be picked up and someone with a big following might tweet it, and on and on it can go.

Aim for quality

Make sure that you put in the effort to make a good-quality video. Use good music, fade-ins and -outs, a lead-in screen with your website address and credits with your web address as well.

There's no need to get the best equipment in the world, but at least use something better than your webcam. The prices of high-definition camcorders (1080p HD) have dropped a lot during the last few years to the point where they are very affordable. And, thanks to royalty-free music and the availability of graphics packages and marketplaces, you can get amazing results while spending only a fraction of what you used to have to spend.

I can recommend the following sites on the Envato network:

- audiojungle.net (*stock music and audio*)
- videohive.net (*motion graphics*)
- graphicriver.net (*graphics, vectors and print*)
- photodune.net (*stock photography*)

Alternatively, just search on Google using some of the italicized terms above.

Do not shy away from controversy

Do you have a product that works better than a competitor's? Can you demonstrate better/faster/cheaper results from your service compared with other companies? If so, create a video of the showdown, but do it with class. You can then target your competitor's keywords as well!

 TIP *Make sure that you have accurate hard data and facts to back up your claims. If you don't, not only will you not convince most of your customers of what you have to say, but you could also find yourself with a libel or defamation lawsuit from your competitors.*

Even if your product or service isn't in itself controversial, you might still be able to link it with a controversial topic, where you argue the case for one side of the argument. If you can find someone from the opposing side willing to discuss the issue with you, you could record yourselves in front of the camera or in a Skype conversation and then upload the resulting video.

- http://skype.com ← *free video and audio calls over the Internet*
- http://www.pamela.biz/en/shop/pamela_call_recorder/ ← *Pamela Software Skype Call Recorder*

Don't discuss religion or politics, unless you are a political or religious site. It may be something that is affecting your business, but mentioning it will immediately turn off half your customers.

Remember that the best videos are fun videos

This point beats all the rest hands down. If you really want something viral, it needs to have a bit of fun in it. This doesn't mean that all your videos need to be fun (a mix of commercial, fun and informational could hit the ticket). But at least some of them have to be fun. If you can't think funny (or at least not funny for everyone), hire a writer from Elance or oDesk.

Put your keywords everywhere

This will help the site and page you are linking to immensely. Do not forget the strategy of deep linking. If you want to promote a dog brush you sell on your website and you make a dog brush video with dog-brush-related keyword tags, title and words in the description, don't add a link in the description to your home page; link it directly to the page on your website that is talking about dog brushes.

Follow the advice given on Monday regarding keyword stuffing. Just make it look natural.

Drive links to your video
As well as linking directly back to pages on your website, it can also benefit you to create a linking campaign for each of your keyword-targeted YouTube videos. There are two main reasons for this:

● Since YouTube is technically the second largest search engine, it's possible to get traffic just by ranking for your keyword on YouTube.
● We know that Google loves videos, and a high-ranking YouTube video is more likely (although not guaranteed) to rank high in the related main Google search index.

Amazon

According to web stats company Alexa, Amazon is the world's largest online retailer and the ninth most trafficked website in the world. You probably already know that they sell everything – from books to treadmills, from engagement rings to flooring – in vast quantities (approximately £9 ($13) billion-worth of sales each quarter).

You could argue that Amazon and other very large commercial websites are in some ways more important than sites like Google, YouTube and Bing. While these three are made up of *searchers* looking for information, maybe before they make a buying decision, Amazon is populated by *buyers*. It's not a search engine; it's literally a buying engine.

If you're a retailer, using Amazon for research is an excellent way to find out about the hot products you should be selling. Just type in a keyword or go to a category, bring up the listing and organize by best-selling/popularity.

Harnessing the power of Amazon

How can you harness the power of Amazon for your own website and business? One obvious way is to write a book giving valuable advice, hints, tips and tricks about your area of expertise. Nothing shouts 'expert' more than having a book for sale on Amazon and it can be used to benefit any type of business, whether it's an e-commerce store, an informational site or a service provider.

E-commerce stores
You could write an instructional guide linked to your products, and include the use of specific products in your store. In the resources section of your guide, you can link back to the product page(s) on your site.

As an example, let's say you have your dog-grooming online store and you want to sell more of your Splentastic 3000 Grooming System. Your idea might be to create a series of books showing people how to groom various breeds of animal. How do you find out whether there is a market for your idea?

1 Go to the top of any page on Amazon and begin typing in the search box and see what comes up. For example, if you start typing 'How to groom a...' Amazon will suggest some search terms people have used, one of which is 'How to groom a Yorkie' (Yorkshire Terrier).
2 If you then go to the Google keyword tool and type in 'How to groom a Yorkie', you'll find 880 exact match searches for that

term. This means that nearly 1,000 people a month, all over the world, are looking for that information. There are plenty of similar search terms that you would have a good chance of ranking your Amazon product page for.

3 If typing that search term into Google brings up no Amazon listings in Google's results and typing it into Amazon brings up only three books, you know that there's a gap in the market.

After writing any book, you can then create an author page on Amazon. Not only does this increase your standing and trustworthiness, but it also lets you link your website or blog to that page. One-way backlinks from super-duper authority site equal SEO gold!

Informational sites

Writing a book focused around your niche or sector is especially good for teaching new people time- and money-saving tips, tricks and techniques, and you can use that book to gain interested visitors to your site. Follow the steps above for research and use the same technique for linking your author page to your website or blog.

Professional/service providers

There is no better form of business card for a professional or service provider than a book. How much more receptive and interested do you think a prospective customer or client would be if, instead of you handing them a business card, you gave them a copy of your book with your phone number in it? Do you think they'd see you as an expert and be more likely to hire you?

If you don't know how to write or put a book together, you can outsource the job; see Saturday.

To get into Amazon, take the following steps.

1 Sign up for an account on Amazon (if you don't have one already) and then go to http://kdp.amazon.com and http://createspace.com and sign up for an account on each of them.
   - Createspace (owned by Amazon) allows you to self-publish and sell physical books that are printed and delivered by Amazon.

- KDP (Kindle Direct Publishing) allows you to digitally
publish and sell your book in Amazon's Kindle store.
2 Take your book, reformat it for the Kindle (you can also
outsource this job and it will definitely save you a world of
hassle) and upload it to your KDP account.

You are now published on Amazon! Now you just have to get
the word out.

You can SEO your Amazon physical and Kindle book pages,
which shouldn't be too difficult since your book title (ideally)
contains a keyword. You can also create a backlinking
campaign for your pages by getting some friends to buy your
book and have them give you reviews.

The key strategy with using books as a marketing tool is *not*
to aim to get rich from book sales; any money you make from
them is a bonus. The primary use for books is as your business
card – as a way for prospects to perceive you as an expert.

There isn't the space here to go into everything to do with
specific marketing tactics with a book, but it is important to
make sure you link your website to your Amazon author page
as well as your YouTube videos and your Facebook page.

Facebook

Facebook is far and away the world's most visited site, not to
mention the largest, with around 5,000,000,000 pages indexed.
No, I didn't put too many zeros there; it is 5 *billion*. The number
of unique pages indexed on just Facebook.com is thus almost
as many as there are people on the planet.

This is why you need to be on Facebook. Regardless of how
you might feel about it and about privacy issues, if you are a
business (and especially if you sell products and services to
private individuals), you need to go where the people are – and
that means Facebook.

Get yourself a personal page, if you don't already have one.
You don't have to share this with everyone, though you probably
do want to start getting more 'social'; remember AuthorRank
and the social signals discussed yesterday.

Get some of your friends to like your page. If you don't have
a lot of friends, run a quick Facebook PPC campaign to get

yourself some likes, which will help other people to like you once they see that other people have.

When you create your Facebook page, take the following steps to link it with your book:

1 Select Brand/product > website, then enter the name of your book.
2 Upload a picture of the book cover as the page's profile image.
3 Fill in the various sections, adding your main website URL and the Amazon page URL, and then follow the instructions in the pop-up boxes.
4 After doing all that, click the 'Edit page' button to go back into your page's settings to see whether you've missed anything.

Making the most of your Facebook page

The don'ts	
In the new timeline layout, don't put any of these in your profile image or cover photo:	• calls to action (for example, 'click here', 'be sure and click like', or even just arrows pointing at the like button) • contact information (even your phone number) • price or purchase information.
For posting on your timeline, don't:	• keep posting the same thing over and over again (this will get you unliked really fast) • post only offers and repeated calls to action (such as 'go here to find out about our amazing offer').
For your cover photo and main image, don't:	• just use stock photos bought from some random stock image site (Facebook needs to be personal and that is not being personal).

The dos	
Always be engaging with your posts. The three posts that get the most engagement are as follows:	• pictures (fun and funny, or shocking and that make you think, depending on your page, of course) • videos (people watch these and love to comment on them) • questions (these have to be well thought out and in line with your website).
When someone writes to you, write back.	• If they answer your question, say thanks and also start a conversation. You will be amazed how fast your page can grow if you take the time to do this.
Be real!	• Don't just say 'Thank you for your post'; comment on the other person's photo or directly address them in some other fashion (or at least have a real person who represents you; see Outsourcing)
Use the apps to connect your other social content to your page. Make sure you put these first and foremost on your page, right under the cover image. The three you must have are:	• YouTube app (puts your YouTube videos in the spotlight) • RSS Graffiti (puts your RSS feed in the spotlight and, by extension, your website) • Fan of the week app (this encourages interactions).
If you have a business that has been around for a while:	• fill in the timeline with your history and milestones by using Facebook's backdating ability • add positive facts such as any awards you received or major clients you landed • use as many images as you can muster. This can show your story in an engaging way that will have people liking and getting to know you; people buy from people they know and trust.

Professional marketer tips

Don't just make one fan page. If you have goods, services or books on Amazon, make a fan page for each of them as well. Use your main fan page to 'like' those pages (and vice versa) and have them all deep-link to your main website to get the maximum linkages for your efforts.

To connect your Amazon book and Facebook the most, create a link in your book directly to an opt-in app on your book's or your company's Facebook. Give visitors a good reason to do this, like offering a free white paper, report or an exclusive discount, and watch as the buyers of your books become customers for life.

Summary

Today you learned that Google isn't everything and that there are other ways to get traffic to start coming to your website. By using YouTube, Facebook and Amazon, you can increase interaction and see traffic growth to your site. Just make sure that you are able to be 'real', be yourself and follow the guidelines of these big social and traffic engines.

You can build on the advice given today to discover the best ways to position yourself to start getting traffic through these giants. So get creative and explore these places. Look at other YouTube videos, Facebook pages and books on Amazon, and feel free to borrow other people's ideas and improve on them!

Also be sure to see what people like. Take note of how many people like a page as opposed to those who dislike it, the reviews a book gets and the interactions of an obviously successful Facebook page.

SUNDAY
MONDAY
TUESDAY
WEDNESDAY
THURSDAY
FRIDAY
SATURDAY

Fact-check [answers at the back]

1. Apart from Google, what other traffic sources are there?
   a) YouTube ❏
   b) Facebook ❏
   c) Amazon ❏
   d) All of the above ❏

2. How big is YouTube in terms of site visits?
   a) Smaller than Bing ❏
   b) Smaller than Amazon ❏
   c) Bigger than Facebook ❏
   d) Bigger than everyone except Google and Facebook ❏

3. What is YouTube ideal for?
   a) Stores ❏
   b) Informational niche sites ❏
   c) Professional services ❏
   d) All of the above ❏

4. Why should you make lots of YouTube videos?
   a) Videos put on YouTube instantly get more Google 'love' than any other video service and often end up in the top ten of Google quickly ❏
   b) They'll make your site look more attractive ❏
   c) You never know what might go viral ❏
   d) Visitors love them ❏

5. Why should you not shy away from controversy when it comes to YouTube videos?
   a) Because it'll catch people's attention and show up your competitors ❏
   b) Because it'll generate publicity and possibly a lawsuit ❏
   c) Because anything goes ❏
   d) Because you'll get more links ❏

6. What are Amazon Kindle books good for?
   a) Professional services ❏
   b) Local businesses ❏
   c) Informational sites ❏
   d) All of the above ❏

7. What is Facebook good for?
   a) Giving out contact information ❏
   b) Giving out purchase information ❏
   c) Links to your main website ❏
   d) Posting the same thing over and over again ❏

8. What should you *not* do on Facebook?
   a) Comment on other people's photos ❏
   b) Use a stock photo as your profile image ❏
   c) Start a conversation ❏
   d) Use as many images as possible ❏

9. Is it good to put a call to action in your cover photo?
   a) Yes, if the action is good ❏
   b) No - it might get you banned ❏
   c) Sometimes, if you have time ❏
   d) What's a call to action? ❏

10. In everything 'social', the most important thing is to be:
    a) Smart ❏
    b) Sneaky ❏
    c) Real ❏
    d) Likeable to everyone ❏

SUNDAY

MONDAY

TUESDAY

WEDNESDAY

THURSDAY

FRIDAY

SATURDAY

Pay-per-click traffic: making it work for you

The purpose of this book is to get you not to rely just on what you are doing today but to have a strategy for the future. Today you will learn how advertising on the Internet can benefit you. This is where you pay money for your visitors, using a method called PPC (pay per click).

Of course, you want traffic that, as far as possible, is free and comes to you naturally, but there are several reasons why PPC should figure in your overall site strategy – at least in the beginning. It's therefore worth discussing here the reasons for doing PPC marketing, so that you don't waste a single penny or minute of your time with it unnecessarily.

Today we'll discuss:

- what PPC marketing is and how it works
- the major players in this arena
- the pros and cons of marketing this way
- the potential costs
- the six situations when you should use this marketing method
- how to set up your successful campaign.

What is pay-per-click marketing?

Pay-per-click (PPC) marketing is a method of advertising on the Internet that is used to direct traffic to websites. Pay-per-click ads usually appear in a coloured box on search results pages, separate from the regular search results. The advertisers pay the publisher (usually a website owner) every time the ad is clicked.

With search engines, advertisers typically bid on keyword phrases relevant to their target market. Content sites commonly charge a fixed price per click rather than using a bidding system. PPC 'display' advertisements, also known as banner ads, are shown on websites or in search engine results with related content that have agreed to show ads.

It should come as no surprise that Google is first on this list. Search and PPC ads are the primary way Google makes its money. When someone types in a keyword, the first two listings on the results page are for ads and all the links on the right-hand side of the page are links to ads. This is Google's Search Network.

Google also has its ads on millions of web pages across the web. This is Google's Display Network. Website owners can apply to Google to have these ads on their web pages via their AdSense program and it's a legitimate way to help monetize a website.

You can learn more about Google's ad networks here: http://adwords.google.com

There are other players in PPC, like Yahoo/Bing, whose ads follow pretty much the same rules as Google, and other, smaller players, but Facebook and Google are where you should focus your effort if you choose this path. To reach the most people fast, it makes sense to use the organizations with the biggest reach.

How does PPC marketing work?

There are two main types of PPC marketing: keyword related and psychographically related. Keyword related is how Google does it in their Search Network. You bid on which keywords your ad will show up on the right-hand side of the search results and you pay the website owner every time your ad is clicked.

PPC and Google

Google is the biggest provider of PPC ads, and you can find out the average cost per click (CPC) for each keyword using either the Google keyword tool or Google's traffic estimator tool (accessible only from within a paid AdWords account). The price you pay is a combination of the amount of competition there is for the keyword and how popular your ad is.

In my PPC campaign, the more times my ad is clicked, the more Google rewards me by – ever so slowly – nudging me up the paid ad rankings. Thus, if my ad was initially placed fourth and ended up getting more clicks than the ads in third, second and first place, it's possible that my ad will jump the queue into first place and, not only that, I'll still be paying the same figure as I was in fourth place.

Once again, Google rewards relevance with ranking and, since ads in first place generally get more clicks than ads in a lower position, you'll get more traffic coming to your website.

Google's Display Network works in a different way:

1 With the Search Network, you're limited to using only text ads. But, because the Display Network is made up of external websites, you can use a text ad, a banner image ad or a video ad.
2 You don't bid on keywords shown up from a search. Instead, you bid to show your ad on pages Google deems relevant to a keyword.

With the Display Network, you can pay either CPC or CPM (cost per mille, the cost per 1,000 impressions – so, when Google shows your ad 1,000 times, you pay the same, regardless of whether your ads are clicked or not).

PPC and Facebook

The second big player here is Facebook. Instead of targeting what people are searching for, you can target people according to their demographic (their age, their sex, etc.) and their psychographic (behavioural) information (e.g. the TV shows, films and products they like).

With Facebook's release of its powerful 'graph search' functionality, there will soon be opportunities for search-related ads on their site. Facebook's own Display Network is also likely to be coming soon, offering further opportunities. For more information, see: http://onforb.es/XaFsEH

Although you can also do demographic targeting in Google, it's nowhere near as detailed as it is in Facebook, because Google simply doesn't have the data. (This is possibly another reason why Google+ was created.) The problem here is that some people don't realize that Facebook has ads. When I mentioned to my mother recently that I was running ads on Facebook, she said, 'Really? Do they have those? Where are they?' so be aware that 'ad blindness' can be an issue.

The advantages of PPC

Using PPC marketing has three main advantages:

● You know that people will probably want what you have.

They went through the trouble and risk of clicking on your ad, so they probably are pretty interested to see what's on the other side.

- You can focus down to the detail for your visitors.
  If you want a specific customer – people from North Dakota who like bubble gum and rock and roll, say – you can definitely find them with Facebook. Google is not quite so refined.
- You can know with almost complete certainty that you will get traffic.

When they're on the ball, Google can approve an ad very quickly. I've personally had ads approved and live in just over ten minutes.

The drawbacks of PPC

The main drawbacks of PPC are the cost and the time required for research and tracking.

1 Costs per click are rising generally and can be unnaturally high.

To reduce costs, you will need to do proper research and point your ads to a specific page (the landing page) on your site, not your home page. Both Facebook and Google are now public companies, answering to shareholders and having to go out of their way to make sure they are profitable. That means that they must extract as much money as possible from advertisers.

Landing page testing

PPC works really well if you're doing any type of landing page testing, as you can find out pretty quickly which landing page is working best.

Keep in mind, though, that you should aim to generate around 200 visitors a day to one or other of your landing page test URLs, so you can find out quickly which page is the best. Then pause this campaign until you need it again, to test the next landing page design against your current champion.

Make sure you set your daily budget high enough to get those 200+ daily visitors.

CPCs can range from anywhere between a few pennies or cents to £30.00 ($50) *per click,* and sometimes more. It all depends on the market and the keywords being bid on. So you really have to do your research into every word you are bidding for to make sure you are getting the amount you can afford. Even this can get really expensive, really fast.

Luckily, both Google and Facebook allow you to set a daily budget limit, so you shouldn't have to sell a kidney or your firstborn to pay your PPC bill. But that daily limit needs to take into account the number of clicks you want sending people to your website.

2 It requires a lot of research and tracking.

Some keywords may be expensive, but they might end up converting less well than other cheaper keywords for you, or vice versa. This is why you need to do research, combined with a lot of tracking. Tracking is where you see where the traffic is coming from and how well it converts (how much they do what you want them to). Compare them to other keywords and narrow down exactly what you need.

When to do PPC

If you're just starting out with a new business and website, you won't have any data to tell you how much to spend on PCC, so just concentrate at this stage on coming up with a compelling offer with a great price. Make a great-looking site and direct traffic to a landing page that presents your offer well (more on landing pages below), and then you will find out whether anyone is interested enough to buy.

Keep track of your results and, as you discover over time how long customers stay with you, you'll be able gradually to increase your spending to acquire new customers.

Don't ever do PPC simply to get visitors to your home page. If you are going to put together a PPC campaign that has any kind of effectiveness, you'll need to make sure that your visitors will have a real reason and purpose for visiting.

Subscription services

You can use a subscription service if you have a product that is purchased by monthly paid subscription, a service to which customers will be loyal or a high-converting, high-value item that hasn't cost you a lot of money. One example of this might be an online business writing press releases for companies, where you have a service supplying a certain amount of material per month, or when you know that, when you write for companies, they tend to stick with you because you do such a good job.

Either way, depending on how much you charge, you now have an idea of how much you can afford to spend to get one customer. This is called the client lifetime value. So, if you charge £49.95 a month for your subscription and you know that a customer will stay with you for an average of 12 months, then the lifetime value of that customer is 12 × £49.95 = £599.40.

Why is this important? When you know how much each customer is worth to you, you can figure out how much you're prepared to spend to acquire each new customer.

High-value items

PCC is also worth doing if you have a high-value or 'big-ticket' item. For example, say you specialize in selling classic Ferraris, and the average profit on each car you sell is at least £7,000 ($10,000). If it costs you 70p ($1) per click to get people to your website and if one out of every 500 visitors buys a car, it might have cost you £350 ($500) to get that new customer, but you still made £6,650 ($9,500) gross profit and you now have them in your customer database, where you can follow up with additional offers for almost no cost.

Social experimentation

PCC could also work in the short term if you need to get a number of people on whom to try out your ideas and see whether they would be worth developing. It's a form of social experimentation as well as an effective marketing method.

For instance, say you are writing an Amazon e-book and you want to know whether people are interested in your subject of hang-gliding in the Andes Mountains. You could put together a little campaign that targets hang-gliding and Andes mountain-related keywords with its title 'Hang-Glide The Andes Mountains?' You can then judge the level of interest by how readily people click on the ad.

You could also put on the landing page a place for people to ask their most burning questions about hang-gliding in the Andes Mountains. Their input will tell you exactly what they will want to see in your book (that isn't even ready yet) and also give you a list of people to email when your book is ready, for a quick burst of sales.

The same theory applies to product retailers and service providers. If people ask the same range of questions before they purchase what you're offering, put up a frequently asked questions (FAQ) page answering them.

Book titles

PCC can also work if you are writing a book and are wondering what the most effective title would be. Take the best ones you have thought of and put them side by side in a PPC campaign. The one that gets the most clicks with the best conversion rate wins! Then, as with social experimentation, you can ask the people who responded what they want to know and get their email addresses.

Niche products

You can also use PPC if you have a small niche product, to get subscribers to your newsletter or RSS feed. This is where you can use the fact that you are a small site to your advantage. I heard about someone who once did a small PPC campaign to their niche bulldog website. It had one focus: getting newsletter subscribers. They spent £20 but ended up with 100 subscribers, several comments on how nice their site was and even a couple of sales.

Facebook sites

As mentioned earlier in the discussion of social media, it is sometimes good to get those first few fans with a quick campaign to target people who will be interested in your page in the first place. For more social media strategies, see below.

PPC advertising strategies

Now you know what you'll focus on, follow these steps on how to set up your PPC ad campaigns.

1 Watch the relevant tutorial videos.

These are provided by Google and Bing to show you the mechanics of creating campaigns and ad groups:

- http://google.com/adwords/onlineclassroom
- http://advertise.bingads.microsoft.com/en-us/new-to-search-marketing

Click the 'Getting started' tab on Bing for even more video tutorials.

2 Plan the structure of your campaigns.

Once you've watched the videos, think about how you'll structure your campaigns on the Google and Bing search networks. The most common way is to use the 'long-tail keyword' approach by creating multiple ad groups, each revolving around a main root keyword and having similar keywords in the same group.

If we go back to the dog-grooming example, and I type in the keyword 'dog grooming' into Google's keyword tool, I'll get a series of keywords all grouped together by theme, as follows:

Kit	Tubs	Clippers
Dog-grooming kit	Dog-grooming tubs	Dog-grooming clippers
Dog-grooming starter kit	Dog-grooming tub	Best dog-grooming clippers
Grooming kits for dogs	Dog-grooming bath tubs	Dog-grooming clippers reviews
Dog-grooming kits for sale	Dog washtub	Wahl dog-grooming clippers
Dog-grooming kits	Dog-grooming tubs for sale	Clippers for dog grooming
	Used dog-grooming tubs	Dog-grooming clippers australia
	Dog bathtub	Best dog clippers
	Dog-grooming baths	Dog-grooming clippers for sale
		Clippers dog grooming
		Dog-grooming clippers uk

3 Transfer your chosen keywords and ad groups to an existing campaign.

Once you've selected the keywords and ad groups you want to use, you can transfer them into an existing campaign in your Google AdWords account (if you're already logged in) with a couple of mouse clicks, by selecting the 'Add to account' button. Bing's process isn't quite as refined as Google's, so what I generally do is use exactly the same keywords and ad grouping in Bing.

If you use the free Google AdWords Editor and Bing Ads Editor software programs, you can easily export your Google campaigns and import them into Bing quickly and easily. Just search in Google for 'Bing Ads Editor' and 'Google AdWords Editor' to get the download links.

Some dos and don'ts

Do:

✔ **set a daily amount you can afford**
Even if it doesn't convert at all, never spend more money than you have budgeted for.

✔ **have an open mind and test out different headlines and bodies of your ads**
See which work out and which don't (this will sometimes be the exact opposite of what you think will happen).

✔ **focus on the *exact* keywords that you want to get clicks on**
The more specific they are, the cheaper and more effective the clicks become.

✔ **point your ad to the right page**
Wherever possible, point an ad to a landing page on your website that is related to your ad.

✔ **always try and get at least an email address for your efforts**

✔ **follow Google's guidelines to the letter.**

Don't:

✗ **make the click go to a one-page website**
This will never be approved by Google and is increasingly not being approved by Facebook. Instead, have it focused on a landing page somewhere in your site where the focus is on what you want them to do.

✗ **make the click go to a page where you can get visitors to click another ad**
This is known as 'arbitrage' and will eventually result in you having your Google AdWords account banned.

✗ **make low-quality landing pages that are not directly relevant to the ad text**
For more information on best practices for landing pages, refer to this guide by Google: http://bit.ly/ReH2nd

✗ **write headlines or body text just to get clicks.**
Clicks are not the point; the point is to get the right people – those who are already interested in what they will get on the other side of your ad.

PPC strategies for Facebook

As mentioned before, Facebook is a different beast from Google in that there are no keywords, as such, to bid to show your ad for. Instead, you need to target people interested in related subjects, located in a certain geographical area, by the college or university they went to, their sex or any other combination of demographic information.

In my experience, the best way to structure your campaigns with Facebook PPC is as follows:

● **Where possible, link your ads to another Facebook page.**
Facebook doesn't really like it when you take people outside Facebook. In my tests, the costs per click of my campaigns halved when I sent people to a Facebook page instead of an external URL.

● **Consider creating a Facebook page for a subject related to your product or service.**
If you intend to run a PPC campaign to generate 'likes' for your company's Facebook page, consider creating a Facebook page for a celebrity or subject that has a broad appeal and is somehow related to your product or service *and then* running a PPC campaign to generate likes for *that* page too. For example, if you were a weight-loss consultant specializing in helping women lose weight and get fit, you might create a fan page around a female celebrity who has successfully lost weight and now looks great (such as Jennifer Hudson if you're in the US or Davina McCall if you're in the UK).

Piggybacking on a celebrity or broad subject like 'weight loss' should make it easier to generate likes for that page, targeting people using your criteria (local area, sex, age, etc.). Then you can send occasional 'promoted posts' to your fans with special offers on your company Facebook page.

If you have a lot of fans/likes for your broad-subject Facebook page, you might be able to sell 'promoted posts' to other companies not in direct competition with you, generating another revenue stream.

Summary

Today you learned that the main uses for PPC are for sales growth (especially big-ticket items and subscriptions) and for testing book titles and book ideas. Make sure you do your keyword research properly and don't just point PPC ads to your home page – you'll end up with high costs per click. When using Facebook PPC, you can get cheaper clicks by pointing to a Facebook page rather than going to an outside website.

Google and Facebook have the power to approve you or disapprove you and your AdWords advertising account. If you are somehow found to be cheating them or their customers, you can be banned for life just as readily as your website. So don't do it.

Make your aim always to find customers/ clients who are already interested in what you have to offer in the first place and you are well on your way to a successful PPC campaign.

SUNDAY

MONDAY

TUESDAY

WEDNESDAY

THURSDAY

FRIDAY

SATURDAY

Fact-check [answers at the back]

1. What does PPC stand for?
   a) Perfectly Politically Correct ❑
   b) Payment Perfectly Considered ❑
   c) Pay Per Click ❑
   d) Panning People Consolidated ❑

2. Who are the main players in PPC?
   a) Facebook ❑
   b) Google ❑
   c) Bing ❑
   d) Everybody else ❑

3. On what should you base a daily limit?
   a) How much you expect to make ❑
   b) Whatever you have in the bank ❑
   c) The size of the market ❑
   d) How much money you can afford to lose ❑

4. What are subscription services?
   a) A good service to use PPC to get clients ❑
   b) A way of driving as much PPC traffic to your site as possible ❑
   c) A high-risk strategy that may or may not work ❑
   d) A complete waste of money ❑

5. In terms of PCC, what's the purpose of your home page?
   a) A good page to use PPC to get clients ❑
   b) A bad idea to drive PPC traffic to ❑
   c) To be the main page for all traffic ❑
   d) To look attractive and draw people in ❑

6. When you do PPC, what should your focus for those clicks be?
   a) Four different options ❑
   b) Three different options ❑
   c) Two different options ❑
   d) One measurable thing that you want them to do ❑

7. Before you start a PPC campaign, what should you know?
   a) Your lifetime client value ❑
   b) How much you are willing to spend ❑
   c) What you want the click to do ❑
   d) All of the above ❑

8. What should you always try to do in your PPC campaign?
   a) Make sales for your efforts ❑
   b) Learn everything about your clients for your efforts ❑
   c) Get at least an email address for your efforts ❑
   d) Have a plan for what to do with the information you glean ❑

9. What are landing pages?
   a) Where the potential client 'lands' after clicking on your ad ❑
   b) One-page sites your clients want to visit ❑
   c) Special pages only for certain users ❑
   d) Website pages run by airlines ❑

10. What should landing pages be?

a) A one-page site with an email address ❑

b) Part of a larger site ❑

c) Interactive, but not too much ❑

d) Pages that immediately take you to another page ❑

SATURDAY

Monitoring and managing your progress

So far, we've talked all about SEO and SEM essentials and some of the small details that you need to make sure you have covered. You've learned about some of the social media giants you need in your traffic-getting strategies, and we've also discussed the possibility and proper use of PPC as part of your online marketing mix.

You may now have begun to feel a little empowered and started dropping jargon and terms left, right and centre into your conversations. You should now be beginning to plan how you will get traffic to your website over the coming weeks and months. You've come a long way over these last few days, but there are a few more points to discuss.

Today you'll find out how to:

- use monitoring software to check your progress up the rankings
- make the job a little easier with some automated tools
- outsource the job completely if you wish, or if you don't have any available staff on hand.

Some of these were mentioned earlier in the week, but they're important enough to discuss again in more detail.

Monitoring software

Now that you have your website up and running and the link 'juice' flowing, the users should be starting to trickle in. How do you know how well you are doing and whether you are progressing or regressing? Now you will learn about the different types of monitoring software out there, free and paid for.

Freeware

Free monitoring software from Google is great to get started with and should be what you go for first, whether or not you want to pay for this assistance later on. You install these tools on your site and they get you aligned with Google.

While they really shouldn't be used by Google to track your site usage or help with ranking, you should assume that they probably are. This is because it's obviously easier for them to track you by just aggregating the data from the free tools already installed on your site without having to send out their spiders and bots all the time.

What to install
Just to be safe, install this first:

● Google Analytics: http://google.com/analytics

This is the online tracking software that shows you how many visitors you have, where they come from (their country of origin), how long they stayed on your site and where they go throughout your site. Go to the page and follow the instructions to install the GA tracking code on every page of your site and you are done. (Hire a geek from oDesk or Elance to do this for you if you're not keen!)

Many of the CMS out there have apps and plug-ins that make this step easy. WordPress has a few plug-ins for adding analytics to your site, including:

- Google Analytics for WordPress: http://yoast.com/wordpress/google-analytics/
- Google Webmaster Tools: http://google.com/webmasters/tools/

This is where Google provides you with reports and data about your website's ranking and the number of pages you have indexed in Google's search engine results. All you have to do is sign up for an account (using an existing or new Google account), add your website URL, verify that you are the real owner of the site and then Google will start crawling and logging data about your site, such as the number of pages it has indexed and which keywords you are showing up for in search results.

To speed things along, you can upload your sitemap.xml file, mentioned earlier. Google Web Toolkit (GWT) will also show what links Google has found that point to your site and whether you have any serious errors on your web page – such as bad code or missing/broken URLs.

TIP *You can even tie your GWT, Google Analytics and Google AdWords accounts together to get optimum data sharing across the various services.*

Be sure to check GWT often, especially in the beginning, to make sure that your SEO efforts are on track. If pages start showing for different keywords from what you were expecting or you start having serious website problems, you'll be able to fix things very quickly.

URL shorteners

URL shorteners are another useful set of tools. These tools include Bitly (bit.ly), TinyURL (http://tinyurl.com), A.GD (http://a.gd) and even Google's own (http://goo.gl).

They will take a really long URL, for example:
http://www.superlongdomainname.org/white/space/florida/songsareawful/end3.html
and turn it into a nice, tidy, short URL, such as:
http://bit.ly/fds8f9

This is especially good for emails, where the long URL would go over multiple lines and possibly 'break' in some email software and where you are restricted to the number of characters you can use, as on Twitter – although they will automatically shorten links with their own *t.co* URL. Some URL-shortening services will also count the number of clicks each link gets if you sign up for an account with them.

There are two things you need to bear in mind with URL shorteners:

1 Emails containing shortened links are being increasingly blocked by ISP.
  This is due to fears that they are spam (unsolicited commercial emails), as a result of high abuse from spammers. For more on this, see this blog post:
  http://blog.wordtothewise.com/2011/06/bitly-gets-you-blocked/

2 Use only URL shorteners that use 301 redirects.
  A 301 redirect is one that tells Google that a page has permanently moved to a new location. So, for instance, if for some reason you are setting up a new domain and have to change the URL
  http://yourdomain.com/yourawesomepage.html
  to this one: http://yournewdomain.com/yourawesomepage.html
  you wouldn't want to lose the SEO benefits from all the links pointing to your old page URL, so you set up a 301 redirect on your old server that tells Google and the other search engines that here is the new URL to use. Once Google and the other search engines know about this permanent redirect, they will pass any SEO benefits from linking to the old page to this new URL.

The same is true for using shortened URLs. If you spend time creating linking campaigns pointing to shortened URLs, you need to make sure that any search engine benefits are passed from your shortened URL to the destination URL on your server, not Bitly's or TinyURL's. Since you don't own Bitly or TinyURL, don't spend time and money getting those domains ranked and not getting yours ranked.

If you don't use an URL shortener that is a 301 redirect, set up your own shortening URL system on a server you control. For WordPress users, there are plug-ins you can use easily to create shortened links on your own domain that will act as 301 redirects. Do a search on the WordPress plug-in repository here: http://wordpress.org/extend/plugins/

Paid-for tools

While the Google Webmaster tools are particularly good, even they – while showing recent changes – don't tell you how you were doing with those keywords months ago.

Here is a list of the tools you can buy that do track your rankings over time:

● Market Samurai ← http://marketsamurai.com
  This all-in-one tool not only tracks how you rank over time but gives you research tools that help you know what keywords to go over. It even promises to tell you exactly what you are missing on your website and what to do to get it to rank.
  Some people find it offers information they don't need but, if you can afford it, get it, because it will tell you pretty much exactly what you need to do.
● Keyword Blaze ← http://keywordblazepro.com
  This tool is mostly a research tool and doesn't tell you what you are missing on your site, but it has many features that automate the process of finding keywords. It even has some features that don't require you to do anything before it pops up and says it has found some related keywords offering you an opportunity.

The rise of third-party services

Back in the old days (before about 2011), if we wanted to see how many links were pointing to a specific page on our website, we would go to Yahoo.com and enter a 'linkdomain:mydomain.com/page.html' command. Although Google had (and still has) a similar command you can use (link:mydomain.com/page.html), it doesn't show all the links pointing to a particular URL. This is to stop people from trying to manipulate the search results.

It was strange to have to go to Yahoo to see how many links we thought were pointing to our pages in Google, but that all changed in 2010 when Yahoo finally retired their Link Explorer function and so third-party services stepped in to take over. Majestic SEO is the biggest and best known of these.

● Majestic SEO ← http://majesticseo.com
Majestic SEO is another excellent tool that is much easier on the pocket. Majestic works in the same way as Yahoo Link Explorer did (see the boxed text above) in that it's a backlink checker that tells you everything you will ever need to know about who is linking to you, and from where. This will show you more about the URLs linking to you than pretty much any other tool. Once you register, you can compare yourself to other sites in your niche, which gives you a clear picture of what you need to do, with many other useful reports and charts.

There is a free account option but, if you can stretch to a paid account, it's worth it.

● SEMRush ← http://semrush.com
This is a suite of tools that covers keyword research, analysis of your competitors and organic search positions for various keywords. It also tries to find any PPC ads by your competitors, with an estimation of what they're spending and the approximate CTR of each ad. It displays SEO data for your site in nice, easy-to-read graphs you can print out.

● SEOMoz ← http://seomoz.org
SEOMoz is another similar suite of tools that gives you excellent data, not only on your own social and SEO efforts

but also on those of your competition. Open Site Explorer will display all links from SEOMoz pointing to the various URLs on your website (just like Majestic SEO), and you can run competitive analyses, get recommendations on how to improve your on-page and off-page SEO and run reports charting your progress.

The role of outsourcing

For you, the business owner, the role of outsourcing is probably one of the most important things you will ever learn – not just in SEO and SEM but also for your business in general. As soon as you can outsource a task, do it, especially if you are the only person in your business. If you try to do absolutely everything, you will slowly burn yourself out and your business – that you've spent blood, sweat and tears building – will suffer.

This book aims to give you the knowledge and understanding you need, so that:

● you know what needs doing and can assign someone else to do it without blindly saying, 'I don't know what I need; just make my website #1.'
● you decrease the chances of being swindled by unscrupulous SEO engineers because you can ask intelligent questions and discover whether they really know what they're talking about.

As you've probably already figured out, the correct setting up of a website is perhaps only 15–20 per cent of the actual work. The constant content creation and the work on SEO are what are going to take time, probably a lot more of your time than you may have previously imagined. This is where outsourcing really comes into its own. You may already be prepared for the need to outsource tech things to do with your website from time to time but, in the long term, if you don't have the time or inclination for doing SEO and SEM yourself, you're going to need someone else to handle it on a permanent basis, and it needs to be done well.

How to scale

Learning how to 'scale' your efforts is learning the art of telling other people how to do things effectively. It's finding that balance between, at one extreme, spending hours going into too much detail and micromanaging every little thing and, at the other, just handing the task to someone and saying 'Get on with it,' while you go off on holiday.

What is missing in both of the above scenarios is:

● having a plan
● projecting the plan.

Follow these steps when delegating, to make sure you get as much out of it as possible:

1 Create a work breakdown structure

This is where you sit down and decide exactly what you want to outsource. Do you want to outsource the content creation, the product selection, the SEO, the SEM, the ad writing, the website techie stuff, or something else? After that, you break down what you want done into a list of smaller tasks.

For SEO, this would include:

● Track progress
● Perform competitive analysis
● Do a weekly backlink check on all web pages on your site, using Majestic SEO or Open Site Explorer
● Find quality links
● Find guest blogging opportunities

 You can find free work breakdown structure templates if you search for them on Google, Yahoo or Bing.

2 Find freelancers and suppliers

Online, great places to find freelancers (people who work for themselves) and suppliers (people who find other people to work for you) are odesk.com, elance.com and freelancer.com. Freelancer recently purchased another large freelancer-type marketplace called Scriptlance, so it's even bigger now.

These websites work like a cross between wanted ads and auction sites. Some of the freelancers on these sites are effectively just suppliers but, either way, they get the job done. You post up the job you want done and freelancers will bid against each other to win the work.

The key to using these sites is to:

- know exactly what you want
  Give as much detail as possible. Don't just say you want someone to build links for you. Look at similar jobs posted up and see how they've been worded. Take what you like from them and craft your own.
- know how much you are willing or able to pay
  On these sites, you can get someone for a pound or two an hour or 100 times as much. If you are not sure how much something you are asking for costs, say so and ask for bids. Remember that you often get what you pay for, so people working for a low hourly rate are not likely to be as good as those asking for more.
- be prepared to pay more for creative tasks
  Graphics and content creation will cost more than technical tasks like building websites or fixing HTML. In my experience there are plenty of great geeks out there, but great writers and graphics people are rare.

Other excellent sources of freelancers include local colleges and universities. Students are always looking for ways to earn some extra money. Placing a request in the student magazine or a postcard on a campus bulletin board or asking for a recommendation from a faculty head might get you a great person you can outsource to. Stay-at-home parents are also another potential source of great freelance staff.

Interview your potential freelancers thoroughly, to make sure that they are the perfect fit and know exactly what you require.

You now have a good idea of what you need to do, but don't necessarily tell a freelancer what you require in exacting detail. Ask them what they think you need; if they give you the right answer, you know they have potential.

3 Manage your freelancers

After hiring your freelancer, have them send reports to you frequently so you can be sure of the quality of their work (especially in areas like SEO), because if they start using tactics Google frowns on, it can hurt your reputation more then it helps!

Whenever I hire a freelancer, I always state in the job specification that I expect daily reports from the beginning. If they don't deliver them, I will cancel the job and let them go. It sounds harsh, but bitter experience has taught me that the maxim of 'Hire slow and fire fast' is true. Your job is not to train them; they are supposed to be the experts before they ask to work for you. That is the definition of a freelancer.

If, after a while, you know that your outsourcer is delivering quality work, you can scale back your checks to once every few days, just to make sure things are going as planned. Then do a thorough review every month to make sure all goals are being met and that your efforts are starting to bear fruit.

Should you hire a project manager?

A project manager is the ultimate compromise between hands-off outsourcing and total task management. A project manager runs everything, including the freelancers, and only tells you about progress, how well things are going and how much money you have made.

Your decision about whether to hire is really a matter of money and time and so, if you have the time to do it, I would recommend doing the job yourself. No one cares about your business as much as you do and it is always difficult to find someone who has the same vision and goals as you do. However, if you really don't have the time or you know that being a manager is just not your thing, this is an option.

Hiring your project manager is your most important hire, though, and you must:

- check and recheck to make sure he or she is invested in the outcome of the project and has a great track record
- make sure all the finances stay under your control: you can never be too careful when it comes to that
- make sure the project manager knows they have to ask before they make any purchases or hires.

Summary

Today you learned about some of the tools that can make the whole SEO process a lot easier. Try them all out if you have time (SEOMoz especially, as they have a 30-day free trial). They can shorten your learning curve considerably and make your experience better. Read my blog for the latest news that could affect you and your business.

You also discovered how to have the work done for you, without spending all your profits in the process, by outsourcing on oDesk, Elance or Freelancer. Use these places wisely to get the best return for your money. Do not hire a project manager unless you really don't have the time and you can easily afford it.

This week you have discovered that SEO is the foundation of marketing on the Internet today. To see real success, you'll need to have a passion for what you are doing, or at least enjoy doing it. Ultimately, it is about making your content good for your user, so keep this always in your mind. Tricks may work for a bit, but true quality – always in short supply – is far more valuable.

SUNDAY
MONDAY
TUESDAY
WEDNESDAY
THURSDAY
FRIDAY
SATURDAY

Fact-check [answers at the back]

1. Which two free tools should you put on every website you own?
   a) Market Samurai and SEMRush ❑
   b) Keyword Blaze and Majestic SEO ❑
   c) SEOMoz and SEMRush ❑
   d) Google Analytics and Google Webmaster ❑

2. What does Market Samurai help with?
   a) Everything ❑
   b) Mainly keyword research ❑
   c) Finding links to you ❑
   d) Automating keyword research ❑

3. What does Keyword Blaze help with?
   a) Everything ❑
   b) Mainly keyword research ❑
   c) Finding links to you ❑
   d) Automating keyword research ❑

4. What does Majestic SEO help with?
   a) Everything ❑
   b) Mainly keyword research ❑
   c) Finding links to you ❑
   d) Automating keyword research ❑

5. What does SEMRush help with?
   a) Everything ❑
   b) Mainly keyword research ❑
   c) Finding links to you ❑
   d) Automating keyword research ❑

6. What percentage of the work is creating your page and finding your keywords?
   a) 50 per cent ❑
   b) 70 per cent ❑
   c) 90 per cent ❑
   d) 10–20 per cent ❑

7. What is a great site for getting contractors for your project?
   a) odesk.com ❑
   b) freelancer.com ❑
   c) scriptlance.com ❑
   d) elance.com ❑

8. When paying low on oDesk, what do you usually get?
   a) The best work ever ❑
   b) Work that's all right ❑
   c) What you paid for ❑
   d) You never know ❑

9. When hiring a freelancer, what should you expect at the beginning?
   a) Daily reports ❑
   b) Weekly reports ❑
   c) Monthly reports ❑
   d) No reports, just frequent questions ❑

10. What does a project manager need?
    a) Complete control ❑
    b) To be micromanaged ❑
    c) Control, but not over finances ❑
    d) The same vision and goals as you ❑

Surviving in tough times

The times are rough, economies all over the world are uncertain; you yourself might find yourself in a difficult situation, with not much money or time to spend on your website to reach your goal of freedom. However, it's never been more important to succeed with SEO and search marketing if you want your site to be accessible to search engines and the wider world, and ultimately to fulfil its purpose. To that end, here are ten tips to help you implement fully what you have found in this book.

1 Do a little bit each day

First and foremost, set time aside time each day to do something with your site. You may find yourself stressed and short of time but don't let this make you put off creating and promoting your site. The tortoise really does win the race, so keep it up and don't compromise on quality. For your site, this could mean putting together just one amazing multimedia experience a month. This is still better than nothing at all.

2 Make maximum use of all the social networks

You probably already use social networks such as Facebook, Twitter and YouTube, so use them for your potential business as well. Commit to one quick post at the beginning and end of each day. Find a fun, interesting or slighty controversial image (do a search on Flickr), or make one yourself using any of the free image-editing software out there. You could also grab related videos from YouTube or use a free screen-capture program or webcam to create one yourself (for example, http://camstudio.org); just make it fun and informative. Then post it to your Facebook page and tweet it.

3 Be social and real

Most of all, to make full use of social networks, have fun and be likeable. At the same time, always use a call to action (ask people to like or share your content). Being real and asking for action will naturally make people want to share both you and your content. To save time in this area, use Hootsuite, a free program that will let you post, tweet and more, all from one website.

4 Design your website well but cheaply

Even if you are doing things on the cheap, you can still use a good-looking theme (free from wordpress.org) for your website. It's not hard to tweak the website options available so that your site looks totally new and unique to you. Even if it doesn't look as perfect as you'd like it, remember that it's your useful and fun content that is more important. As long as your website design is good enough not to distract your customers, you should be fine (at least at the start). Pay for a smarter design later, once you've made your cash.

5 Use plug-ins

Since you are using WordPress, use as many high-rated plug-ins as you can find to make your life as easy as possible. Do not go overboard and try to automate everything (because, at the end of the day, manual is best). For some excellent free and low-cost plug-ins, search on Google for 'top 10 essential WordPress plug-ins'.

6 Make good use of your keyword selection time

One thing you shouldn't skimp either time or effort on is your keyword search time. Set aside a whole day, or two if you have to. Lock yourself in a room and focus. During this time, create a detailed plan that will be good for months or even years (you might just create one good piece of content a month). To do this more cheaply, time your research using a paid tool during its intro period when it's free, remembering to cancel before the monthly fee kicks in.

7 Specialize as much as possible

Do not try to sell everything in the world in an effort to make money. Making your offer too broad may ultimately lead to you making little or nothing. When doing your keyword research, your best bet is to define your niche clearly, making it as specific as possible, while generating enough searches every month to keep it profitable.

8 Link-build naturally

Build your links naturally by being active in your niche. Create profiles on Google Plus for author rank and tie everything to your name. Find good, solid, non-competing but related blogs on blogcatalogue.com and start adding value and comments using your name and your website. After getting good content on your site, sign up to be a guest writer on postrunner.com and other related sites. You can also hire someone cheaply on oDesk to email other related blogs/websites constantly to get you on those as well.

9 Avoid PPC – if you don't have the budget

If you are short of cash, don't use PPC or any other paid traffic. Doing this the wrong way can mean that you will be in debt to Google and others, and that can only hurt your efforts in the long run. The sole reason for using PPC at this stage would be to test your landing page to ensure that it converts. Be sure to turn it off as soon as you hit your limit, though. Use PPC marketing only after you are making some money from your sites.

10 Watch out for 'shiny object syndrome'

As you start to promote your company online, you'll begin to be inundated by dozens, even hundreds, of ideas, tips and tools that promise instant 'push-button' traffic to your website. Ignore these, and keep things simple to start with. Find what works for you to create good material and keep going with that until you succeed. Don't be distracted by the latest trend, to the detriment of creating fun posts and content. The latest shiny tool or website may be cool, but don't become a technique or software collector without also being a content-generating machine.

Spend 90 per cent of your time using what you know will work – and spend the other 10 per cent testing new ideas.

Answers

Sunday: 1c; 2d; 3c; 4a; 5c; 6a;
7d; 8d; 9a; 10d.

Monday: 1b; 2d; 3a; 4c; 5b; 6d;
7b; 8a; 9d; 10d.

Tuesday: 1b; 2c; 3b; 4a; 5d; 6c;
7d; 8d; 9a & b; 10b.

Wednesday: 1d; 2b; 3b; 4b; 5d;
6b & d; 7c; 8b; 9a & b; 10d.

Thursday: 1d; 2d; 3d; 4a & c; 5a;
6d; 7c; 8b; 9b; 10c.

Friday: 1c; 2a & b; 3d; 4a; 5b; 6d;
7d; 8c & d; 9a; 10b & c.

Saturday: 1d; 2a; 3b; 4c; 5d; 6d;
7a, b & d; 8c; 9a; 10c.

ALSO AVAILABLE IN THE 'IN A WEEK' SERIES

ALSO AVAILABLE IN THE 'IN A WEEK' SERIES

For information about other titles
in the series, please visit
www.inaweek.co.uk